The Golden Bird

The Golden Bird

New and selected poems by

ROBERT ADAMSON

Black Inc.

Published by Black Inc.,
an imprint of Schwartz Media Pty Ltd
Level 5, 289 Flinders Lane
Melbourne Victoria 3000 Australia
email: enquiries@blackincbooks.com
http://www.blackincbooks.com

The National Library of Australia Cataloguing-in-Publication entry:

Adamson, Robert, 1943-
The golden bird : new and selected poems / Robert Adamson.
9781863952873 (pbk.)
Includes index.

A821.3

Book design by Thomas Deverall

CONTENTS

A FUTURE BOOK

This book is for Juno, always

A Bend in the Euphrates

In a dream on a sheet of paper I saw
a pencil drawing of lovers: they seemed perfect,

Adam and Eve possibly. Stepping into reality,
I read lines of a poem on a piece

of crumpled rag I kept trying to smooth—Egyptian
linen, so fine it puzzled to imagine such a delicate

loom. In a flash I saw two dirty-breasted ibis
and heard their heads swish: black bills

swiped the cloudy stream, and in the rushes
I heard needles stitching, weaving features

into the landscape, clacking as they shaped
an orange tree, then switched a beat to invent

blue-black feathers for crows, the pointed
wedges of their beaks. A fox rustles

through wild lantana as I step through into
the garden and, becoming part of the weave,

notice the tide turn, its weight eroding mudbanks,
bringing filth in from the ocean. A raft of flotsam

breaks away, a duckling perched on the thicket
of its hump. I use the murky river for my ink,

draw bearings on the piece of cloth, sketch
a pair of cattle egrets bullying teal into flight.

The map's folded away, I travel by heart now,
old lessons are useless. I shelter from bad weather

in the oyster farmer's shack. The moon falls in a
column of light, a glowing epicycle—

this pale wandering spot on my writing table
these fragments of regret:

DREAMING UP MOTHER

جرہ

Where I come from, the belated homework

Green Prawn Map

♪ In memory of my grandfather H.T. Adamson

Morning before sunrise, sheets of dark air
    hang from nowhere in the sky.
No stars there, only here is river.

    His line threads through a berley trail,
a thread his life. There's no wind
    in the world and darkness is a smell alive

    with itself. He flicks
a torch, a paper map *Hawkesbury River*
    & District damp, opened out. No sound
but a black chuckle

    as fingers turn the limp page.
Memory tracks its fragments, its thousand winds,
    shoals and creeks, collapsed shacks

a white gap, mudflats—web over web
    lace-ball in brain's meridian.
This paper's no map, what are its lines

    as flashlight conjures a code
from a page of light, a spider's a total blank?
    So he steers upstream now

away from map-reason, no direction to take
    but hands and boat to the place
where he will kill prawns, mesh and scoop

in creek and bay and take
his bait kicking green out from this translucent
    morning.

    Flint & Steel shines
behind him, light comes in from everywhere,
    prawns are peeled alive.

Set rods, tips curve along tide, the prawns howl
    into the breeze, marking the page.
He's alone as he does this kind of work—

        his face hardened in sun, hands
moving in and out of water and his life.

My House

My mother lives in a house
where nobody has ever died

she surrounds herself
and her family with light

each time I go home
I feel she is washing
and ironing the clothes of death

these clothes for work
and for going out
to the Club on Sunday
and for Jenny to take her baby
to the doctor in

death comes on the television
and Mum laughs

saying there's death again
I must get those jeans taken up

My Granny

When my granny was dying
I'd go into her bedroom
and look at her

she'd tell me to get out of it
leave this foul river

it will wear you out too

she was very sick
and her red curly hair
was matted and smelt of gin

sometimes I sat there all day
listening to the races
and put bets on for her at the shop

and I sat there the afternoon
she died and heard her say her last words
I sat there not telling

maybe three hours
beside the first dead person I'd seen

I tried to drink some of her gin
it made me throw up on the bed
then I left her

she said the prawns will eat you
when you die on the Hawkesbury River

My Tenth Birthday

We went to Pumpkin Point
for my tenth birthday

the best picnic beach on the river

the mud is thinner
and doesn't smell as off

and there is a swing
made from a huge truck tyre

I wore my first jeans
and got a cane rod and a bird book

Dad washed the rabbit blood
out of the back of his truck
and we spread blankets
and pillows over the splinters

A storm came up after lunch
and I cut my foot open
on a sardine can as I ran into a cave

it was the same cave
I found again four years later
on a night my father set out the nets

and slept beside me
for the only time in his life

The Harbour Bridge

I went with Dad on the sulky
into town across the Harbour Bridge

it was a windy cold day

I wasn't too keen on going
along in a horse and cart in the city

I slid down under the seat
so the horse's tail swished in my face

we passed trams and women
standing at the crossings

and Dad just driving through it all
as if he was still up the river

his hat on his head
and his son beside him
with the city grit getting on me

the shopping growing in the back
beans and tomato trees

the blood and bone spilling behind us

My Fishing Boat

Mum and Dad are at it again
in the room
next to mine
their terrible sobbing
comes through the damp wall

they fight about something
I have done

I get out of bed
and go down the yard to the river
push my boat out into
the black and freezing bay

under the mangroves
that smell like human shit

I move along my secret channel
my hands blistered
from rowing slip with blood
around the cove I tie up on a mangrove
it rains harder

all I catch are catfish here
and have them sliding
about in the belly of the boat

they are the ugliest-looking things
in the world

My First Proper Girlfriend

The first girl I wanted to marry
was Joan Hunter
her father owned more oyster leases
than anyone else on the river

she had buck teeth
but she looked okay really

we'd sit on her father's wharf
and watch the mullet together for hours

they will take over the world one day

we loved each other alright

my parents hated us being together
and called her Bugs Bunny

One night my father cut Joan's dad
with a fishing knife
right down his left cheek

that little Protestant bludger
with his stuck-up bitch of a daughter

Growing up Alone

1

Walking down our backyard
scraping my legs on blackberries

at the steps I pull on the ropes
holding up the old twine
gill-net used for
trapping starlings now

they hit it
then flap out
until they strangle themselves
the same as mullet

I tear out the birds at eye level
ripping the weak mesh
and throw the bodies onto the compost

its heap spreading down
to the tide-line
putrescence curling out
from the warm centre where blowflies

cluster in the thick of it

2

Me and Sandy would go
out onto the mudflats at low tide
catching soldier crabs

we'd talk about what would happen
if she ever got pregnant to me

because we were first cousins
our baby would have
one of those big heads

and maybe no hand or something

3

Sandy was pretty ugly too

blotched freckles on her screwed-up face
skinny legs and no tits

good hair though
curly and real yellow

she always had cold sores on her lips
that tasted salty

4

At midday I'd walk to the Point
and there'd be nobody

I'd look at the starlings
the only things that could take it
hard birds that shine

eating anything just about
one day I watched them get through a cat
that'd been run over

it took them a morning

5

Sandy knew a place at Cheero Point
where we'd go behind a tree
and stare into the eyes of God

they were in the face
of an old yellow cat who'd gone mad

once we looked we wouldn't be able to move
sitting there for hours sometimes
before it let us go

6

The backyard to our grandfather's
was the Hawkesbury River

and me and Sandy hated it
It meant all the kids at Gosford
knew how poor we were

because only fishermen lived there
and we hated it because

when you went out on it at night
the dark was frightening
and the ground was full of ants

the river with its savage tides
that would wear you out in half an hour

and in summer the heat
and sun burning into your neck

giving you awful headaches
and nothing to do but fish or hide

7

I'd been crying under the house

I ran out onto the road
into the same dust and heat again

with the lousy starlings
the dark sheen on their wings
oily metallic green

I thought about the way we die

the steps just falling away
from under me as I ran

the heads of jewfish
nailed out along the wharf rail

two hundred and seven
some skulls and others still flesh

all with their eyes eaten out

8

I had this game it was all different
the papershop wasn't neat

and the pub didn't smell so rotten

I'd sit in Dad's truck and look out
at the town's light
a clear steady light
nothing like the river's

softer and shifting
and with people walking through it

9

Along the shore in the mud
I'd walk all day alone

and wonder how come nothing
ever happened

how come I didn't go mad or something

mud caked all over me
and my face throbbing with sun

and never seeing anyone

10

We cover our faces with mud
and become hunters
in the mangroves barefoot and nude
our arms sting from cuts

we talk less until we only make sounds

Sandy gets the first bird
an old wood duck
we share its feathers on the run

then onto the mudflats
our feet sinking in four feet of mud
where the big crabs swim

out here branches rot away
and we pull each other
up out of the mud by our hair

soon you don't feel things
and you have to get back to the rocks

before you realise what you've
been doing all day

Coda

Fishing skiff in the light
at Mackerel Flats, mud-caked, sun borne
by the old man caulking cracks.

Rust scales drop from boat-slip
to silt as he moves.

Gnawed, hacked heads of black bream
rock through the wash.

Skeleton trophies, Banjo Rays,
staked out on a pile,
their whip tails paralysed chalk.

Light seeps through folds in his turkey neck—
his eyes don't blink

and flick out involuntarily to where
mud-gudgers pick at the heads.

He is alone with his tinkering work.

He holds the scraper
like a little axe and chips
away at the belly of his boat,
his finger flesh grown over
his fingernails, his hair freckled white,
his pupils contracted points.

It is morning
and the mangrove air is sweet

as I move toward him, my leather shoes
cracking oyster grit.

I ask how's the fishing
my alien voice reminding me
he is the grandfather of what I am.

Mulberry Leaves

Out the back in the kitchen, my mother
chops through root vegetables, filleting mullet,
threading our meals together. My father stokes
a fire in the yard, boiling up offal and fish frames
in a forty-four-gallon drum; a mist rises from his
liquid fertiliser baked all day in the sun,
clinging to us and the windless air.

The heat hangs around after dark.
Steam fogs the glass of a pressure lamp
hissing yellow light from a fragile mantle.
The country music station plays softly.

Dad sings along with Hank Williams as he works.
He takes a slug of his home brew and coughs
until he lights another smoke. My hands
are full of mulberry leaves and silkworms,
their yellowish cocoons seeping transparent
blood from injured larvae. Inside my
cardboard shoe box, God laughs on.

Father's Day

I cart home sugarbags of coke from the gasworks.
My hands smudge the cream-painted icebox. My father
throws spuds on the fire, sending sparks up the flue.

On the hill outside, trucks growl and strip their gears.
I imagine the peach-faced finches of Madagascar.
After tea, Dad slumps in his chair, tall brown bottles

standing empty on the table. At school each day I fail
my tests. My mother's face hardens when I try to speak.
She irons starch into my sister, from her straight black

hair to her school uniform's box-pleats. In the backyard,
cuckoo chicks squawk from a magpie's nest. The hedge
man's finished clipping the hedges along our street.

My brothers bob down to do their homework, into
the learning stream, heading for their lives,
biting the heads off words.

Drum of Fire

Out the back my father's burning off—
drums of scrap, the lead casing
dripping from the copper wire,
toxic black smoke billowing into the air
each weekend, the lead trickling
down, molten rivulets spitting fire,
becoming deformed ingots. His
fuming shadow looming over
neat rows of vegetables.
In dreams I went back to school at night,
cutting through the alphabet,
torching examination papers, drunk
on fumes of kerosene, my fingers
marking strokes. At morning
assembly we sang the national anthem flat
with deadpan faces—I blew
into a flute for a whole term but wept
each night over my arithmetic
homework—then down to the Police Boys
boxing with the bigger kids until my
eyebrow bled too much. In the park
I flew with rainbow lorikeets
and hung upside down in the branches
of flowering coral trees. I sucked
nectar with them and stole their feathers;

prowled back lanes with a pair
of parrot's claws dried into spiky stars
in my pockets. Back home I'd stare
into my father's drum of flames—
conjuring images of the new Ford Thunderbirds
that came purring through our suburb,
and found no meaning in my father's fire
as he stashed another ton of scrap copper wire.

The Mullet Run

Gone for days, and way down the river—
an old man? We sat around the Angler's Rest
playing the jukebox: Slim Dusty
saving us from talk. I played with my

rum & Coke. We were home by midnight, walked
all the way to Mooney, and Christ,
where was he, as if I didn't know. I slept on
the verandah to overlook a slackening tide.

3 a.m. my cousin came back to say
she loved me—soon I would explore my sensual
dream, and Sandy's beery breath—like
I'd planned all those months. A southerly,

of course, blew up just before dawn, ripping
canvas from the window frames; branches
snapped clean off the mulberry tree
to fall across the bed. Our calico

sheets were soaked with rain and sticky dark
stains. Almost half the rusty
corrugated iron blew from the roof,
and, really, what could've I done? Wind dropped,

dawn, sun in the slanting mulberry tree.
It was midday before our grandfather
finally got back. We heard his boat down beside
the wharf—I stayed in the house

pretending to clean up. By the time he came
through the front door, saw the roof half gone,
and said there'd been a mullet run,
we knew somehow he didn't want to know.

I couldn't have told him then, but needed him
to ask. We just followed him down
to his trawler, helping to pack mullet into
boxes of crushed ice. Sandy was the first to go,

she just dropped everything and ran.
I knew he didn't really want me there,
but held on for a while at any rate—and then
filled a kero tin with mullet gut,

carried it up the yard, and sat there an hour
feeding it to his chooks. The scales curling in the sun,
falling from my arms.

Dead Horse Bay

Quick hands on spinning ropes
at dawn, blood rising
to the jumping cords,

ice-packs over bad burns
and the catfish venom,
rock salt against gut-slime,

a southerly blowing up
on the full tide, nets
in mud and mesh-gutting snags,

the bread tasting
like kero-sponge, crazed gulls
crashing onto the stern

and mullet at three cents a pound
by the time the sun hits the bar
at the Angler's Rest.

Get drunk enough to keep at it,
clean the gear for tonight
and another bash.

Remember that night in '68
how we killed 'em
right through the month

couldn't have gone wrong,
so thick you could've
walked over the water.

When the bream are running
like that, nothing can touch you
and everything matters

and you don't want 'em to stop
and you can't slow down
you can't imagine.

Dreaming up Mother

Understanding is all, my mother would tell me,
and then walk away from the water;

Understanding is nothing I think, as I mumble
embellished phrases of what's left of her story.

Though I keep battering myself against the sky,
throwing my body into the open day.

Landscapes are to look at, they taught me,
but now the last of the relatives are dead.

Where do these walks by the shore take us
she would say, wanting to clean up,

after the picnic, after the nonsense.
I have been a bother all the years from my birth.

Look out—the river pulls through the day
and Understanding like a flaming cloud, goes by.

THE REBEL ANGEL

Cars, drugs, reform school, prison

from The Imitator

Dirty hypodermics rattle in the glove box—
morphine flows over the top of your brain—
an artery collapses—migraine floats out of your eyes.
Alright, there'll always be glib explanations:
cashing in on experience again?

Don't be distracted now, watch the speedo,
plant your foot until the big V8 starts
to mainline juice straight from your cirrhotic
liver—let her go, the most fantastic demo ever.
Lowflying through suburban hills, taking

red lights at sixty-five, hoping for some brickwall
overdose to bash your head against,
until a piston snaps its rings and cracks the block—
but there's only a missing spark and kick
back from screwing in the dark. Don't freak now,

come down slow with codeine phosphate;
speed as much as you like, just hang on
to your impetus and never use the brake.
Keep shooting and you'll find there's no right
side to the double yellow lines—Make sure

the windscreen's always clean, don't read traffic
signs unless you've passed them once before.
When the morphine goes to water, move on
with heroin—shoot up with quality.
Stay clear of bikeboys, hoods and Chinamen—

use anything, stay numb as long as you can,
any pain now could be deadly, they'll sense it,
knife in, and you're gone—Care for your
Customline's your habit, and you're on your own.

The Rebel Angel

Shit off with this fake dome of a life, why
        should I remain here locked in my own
buckling cells? So there's always
        a way round the city mornings when parks
are lakes of smouldering green—
        & there's a way as you're blown along
by some black vision of a cop that's
        nagging inside your gut—
you know so well the way that'll carry you back:
        follow a railway line

studded with muck-green stations
        & bubblers spouting lukewarm water— No,
you've left it too late & now there's
        cold weather coming along &
a pile of junk in your brain—These days it's
        risky to drive after midnight.
It's slowing you down always looking behind
        all the time getting someone to pluck
down the blinds—So now as you spin
        through a drunk there's lots of reasons

why you have to stay put—reasons that say
        you can't piss off anymore from
serving two and a half years straight: of knowing
        it's lights out at ten every night,
the sleepless lays churning in your bunk
        until each counted dawn, of singing
without sound—I've looked around every inch
        of the jail & dug my own groove in yellow
sandstone, & searched without sleep
        & searched again

back on the street in the rain—searched for
        some kind of rebel angel,
                        some kind of law.

Passing through Experiences

I lived on drugs and understood the pushers
As the crackup came on
There was nobody to blame and I confessed for hours
Until the police were in tears

The prison had a few prophets but they
Understood themselves
During the night the lucky ones burnt their tobacco
Each morning I feigned silence

The experience of prison remained behind bars
I dwelt on the idea of freedom
And folding *The Prince* away when afternoon appeared
Went after pain

The ideas crowded around like pushers
And fed on my doings
I discovered thought as powerful as cocaine in winter
As a screw off-duty I tapped my foot

All experience pointed to Saint Theresa
The Prince reassured me
I escaped from the books but names kept coming up
Pain alone said nothing great

I ask her why you know it all though say nothing
Believe me pain replies You don't falter
You move

The Beautiful Season

Some sunny day does not support more
reason than a dull one; green lights
from the harbour still remind us of a tour
through Spain. Two whistling-kites

are fishing in a shallow day: even birds
would not support a proper reason
for the inclusion of corroborated words.
A sample of the beautiful season

came wrapped in aluminium foil: oh cute
as a new drug—but let's remember
how the most vicious thug wore silk suits
and plugged sparrows in December.

The sunny day is no more 'cute' than a drug
in foil; lights on water are seldom
memories. Our bird-loving thug
has returned muttering 'O Kingdoms'

Some More Experiences

Seems we were born in captivity, he said, and burn
Our curious lives out in these slow states
Numbered by the days; who knows? My lover's turn
Coat mind turns about, dreaming of the gates.

And he forgets me easily behind the yellow walls.
He's been round on the outer—screws
Tell me he's even got a wife who calls
The Commissioner every day for some news

Of his release. (As if they'd know—
They bitch me many ways.) All night he talks
And holds me, all night he loves me slow
And careful. The screws pace the catwalks—

In time their footsteps mark our love.
Who, now, can really know him more than me?
Once he hugged me till my bones were sore—
We understood the terror then in being free.

Seems we should be born in captivity, I said; love
Might hold our curious lives in some new lore.
Oh, yeah, he said, whatever you reckon—
Love's a lagging in a way, whatever you reckon.

Action Would Kill It / A Gamble

When I couldn't he always discussed things.
His talk drew us together:
the government's new war, the best French brandies
and breaking the laws. And it seemed
a strange thing for us to be doing,
the surf right up the beach, wetting our
feet each wave

on that isolated part of the coast, counting over
the youngest politicians.
Huge shoulders of granite grew higher
as we walked on, cutting us from perspectives.
He swung his arms and kicked
lumps of quartz hard with bare feet,
until I asked him to stop it ...

He didn't care about himself at all, and the sea
just licked his blood away.
The seemingly endless beach held us firm;
we walked and walked all day
until it was dark. The wind dropped off and the surf
flattened out, as silence grew round
us in the darkness.

We moved on, close together, almost touching.
He wouldn't have noticed; our
walk covered time rather than distance.
When the beach ended,
we would have to split up. And as he spoke
clearly and without emotion
about the need for action, about killing people,
I wanted him.

Angel's Own Kind

1. Ram lives

Spun round on his boot heel, turned to face
the enemy, 'Be told you bastard, just
be told,' but he would not be told. A shotgun
bucked and bodies slapped across a parking lot.

The beer garden a zone of transformation
fear zig-zagged with death along the ground,
tar pocked with glass and flesh, the killers
now as ugly as their words. The 'enemy'

had disappeared, gone without a trace, were
never there, invisible to drinkers
and to police. The words 'be told' had left

their speaker flat, a heap of leather
and torn fleece. His wife and daughter there,
Ram's witnesses, pushed beyond belief.

2. Law of the land

Her best friend said, 'Don't listen and don't go,'
but she had to know. The emblems a silver fire
spelling the mystic names: *Norton, Harley
Indian*—Her fascination part fear, part desire.

She dreamed of flying low through fields
of floating wheat, to come alive,
her lover's bike a motor hooked to the universe.
She saw the Lost Highway to the Lake—

She was a world away from 'Don't listen
and don't go' when a noise in the car park
shook her from her dreaming—she looked out,

her friend waved from the bar—
She heard bullets rip the air, then saw the flecks
of Ram's brain splattered across the tar.

3. Last rites

Their club rode out through country towns,
dreams becoming real—they stopped
at pubs, swam in streams—shot rabbits
in paddocks of grazing sheep. Breathing

petrol fumes and country air. Almost thirty
strong, the land stretched on, their bikes roared
and they sang in a language of their own—
She smiled, this was her dream, her hair

wild in the wind, the motor perfect
in its heat—they wheeled in through suburbs
then pulled into the Road Warrior's Hotel.

Don't listen, be told, don't go, you bastard—
In the beer garden at night this old refrain,
then the stars ripped down onto that slab of tar.

Things Going out of My Life

The things that are going out of my life remain
in its wake a few yards

behind following me asking to be retrieved like
cigarette packets bobbing
at the stern of a boat leaving
with the tide

And it seldom occurs to me that they are not in
the water but could be falling
from my life

as it rises up from earth
or tumbling haphazardly downhill after me
These things leaving

often ask to be identified even though they know
it would be impossible

When I wake up mornings alone it is more disturbing
when I imagine it could be
the living things
that are going out of my life

Not a Penny Sonnets

∿ Remember the club sandwich? —GIG RYAN

I.

A book launch, plates of water biscuits.
'There's always the club sandwich,' you said.
But the corporate types didn't get it—they were
busy being freaks—so we spliced letters into words
as verbal tattoos, using anything we'd written,
digging our biros in. A girl drives by
in a low-slung Torana. Remember the suburbs,
those days of ordinary defeat? Using street directories
so out of date they didn't have new streets?
We had dreams of driving racing cars. These days
we can afford to trade quips at the Intercontinental,
go to funerals, throw out old affections. Drinking
beer and double gins, I'm talking
but nothing seems to grip.

2.

I've written my response before you speak:
'Well, fiddle-de-dee,' we said to the police,
walking onto the illuminated page,
being freaks, digging our biros in. We honed
our beaks on cuttlefish bones from your baptismal
swim, stringing along the corporate types, filling
shot glasses to the brim in our separate skins.
Cracks? Take a bite and your teeth might ache

with old affections and lost destinations.
We sharpened the edge for decades, drinking hard,
looking for something to blame. Remember smoking
ready-makes? You demanded things—impossible—
from me. I had nothing, not a penny to my name,
just references, chips, and lemonade.

3.

We scoff at good luck from the Intercontinental,
flash Medicare cards before signing anything.
Our biros dig in to *Gone with the Wind*, breathing
air-conditioned memories in separate skins—
goose pimples, anti-fashion, enemies, and friends.
Back on the street, we take in the city.
A Torana spins its wheels, skeins of brown smoke
clog the pavement—she's gone. But we're still
standing here, talking, destroying words.
The club sandwich? Well, fiddle-de-dee. We believe
nothing: the shredded trust, the corporate types—
just limping figures in dressed skin. The life
we mocked surrounds us—distracted,
but the tide keeps coming in.

THE GATHERING LIGHT

ॐ

Ah, Wordsworth, why were you so human?

Meaning

A black summer night, no moon, the thick air
drenched with honeysuckle and swamp gum.

      In a pool of yellow torchlight
on a knife-blade, the brand name
                            Hickey Miffle—
I give in to meaninglessness, look up
try to read smudges of ink
                    a live squid squirts
across the seats—now the smell of the river hones
an edge inside my brain,
      the night sky, Mallarmé's first drafts.

Who can I talk to now that you have left
the land of the living? The sound of more words.

The moon rolls out from the side of a mountain
and I decide to earn the rent;

      the net pours into a thick chop,
a line of green fire running before the moon's light—

Does four-inch mesh have anything to say tonight?

The mulloway might think so if they could—
Ah, Wordsworth, why were you so human?

      On Friday nights I fork out comfort,
but tonight I work with holes, with absence.

I feed out a half-mile of mesh pulling the oars;
this comes once a life, a song without words
    a human spider spinning a death web

across the bay. Alcohol, my friend my dark perversion,
here's to your damage:
    who do you think you are?

My mother the belly dancer, my father Silence,
    my house that repeats itself wherever I go.

The Night Heron

Midnight, my mind's full of ink tonight,
I'm drawing up some endings to make
a few last marks. Life's complete.
You're just part of the mix,
a pain cocktail, a dash of white spirit,
some pulvules of dextropropoxyphene
swallowed with black label
apple juice, as I cut and paste my past.

Life is sweet. Out there the night,
the stars in technicolour, a half-moon—
two half-moons, the black branches
of a mangrove tree. Jasmine's
heavy in the hot air, I feel alright
even here suspended in a humid room
with another summer to get through.
I write down words, they all seem fake,

so I crack them open. A night
writing letters to the future and the past—
if you could look into the present
you might see this pudgy figure at the desk
throwing back double shots of gin,
fumbling for cigarettes and a light
writing the word 'political' in a black
thin calligraphy. Wearing a pair of digital

blinkers set on zero. Outside the night
heron swings in from the heavens
and cuts through the aluminium light—
see its cream underwings, the grey breast,
the tan overcoat, watch it hit the pocket
of hot air, listen as it wheels on silence,
glides into the black calm above the swamp
and lands collecting in the creek.

The White Abyss

After a life, the next decade
is a concept I must comprehend—
Time, wrote Augustine, is some kind of trick.

He asked his God to forgive him
for thinking along these lines,
it had to be done.

What happens next? Outside
Hell smoulders as usual
inside, electricity and words.

Everything exists to end in the book.

I live in Mallarmé's head for days
nothing happens and this
is paradise, thoughts
unfold instead of flowers, abstract and warm.

I have not experienced a grief
as devastating as the black abyss
the death of Anatole left—
this is a corner of the head I prefer
not to revisit

when I go back the intensity
of the experience of loss leaves me empty.

This is death then, a blank
where no thought flowers, a pit of black
tideless water, where no fish kill.

Here you realise you can live through anything,
stripped, without a head, your soul
shown up for the joke souls are.

Then you begin to understand Augustine.

The Gathering Light

Morning shines on the cowling of the Yamaha
locked onto the stern of the boat,
spears of light shoot away
from the gun-metal grey enamel.
Now I wait for God to show
instead of calling him a liar.

I've just killed a mulloway—
it's eighty-five pounds, twenty years old—
the huge mauve-silver body trembles in the hull.

Time whistles around us, an invisible
flood tide that I let go
while I take in what I have done.
It wasn't a fight, I was drawn to this moment.
The physical world drains away
into a golden calm.

The sun is a hole in the sky, a porthole—
you can see turbulence out there,
the old wheeling colours and their dark forces—
but here on the surface of the river
where I cradle the great fish in my arms
and smell its pungent death, a peace
I've never known before—a luminous absence
of time, pain, sex, thought, of everything
but the light.

Tropic Bird

ᔧ *Lord Howe Island*

Wakes from nimbus cut to streaks
by the clipped volcanic peaks
mingle with an orange sky, the colour
of parrot-fish gut. Monsoon

time, nothing's quite right,
people drink or sleep or drift about.
On my deckchair's arm a tumbler
of gin has sucked in a dragonfly.

I drink myself sober as they say.
All that happens is my past
oozes through its pack of black jokes
and disasters. During *Under the Volcano*

I sucked bourbon through a straw
from a milkshake carton, at 4 a.m.
eating handfuls of ice-cream
I tried to soothe a hangover that went on

for a decade. I watched three
Siamese cats and as many marriages
sink with the fish. Always fish.
Tight water in black pools, moonlight

etching outlines of game-fishing boats
onto my brain—moored in slots,
fat with money yet taut, their
trimmings set to kill. I worked them,

sharpened hooks for high-rollers,
sewing my special rigs—
bridles for bonito, live bait that
trailed the barbed viridian in our wake.

On the arm of my bamboo chair the glass
of gin is blossoming. The sky opens
and in sails, on black-edged wings,
a white, gracefully inhuman, tropic bird.

Thinking of Eurydice at Midnight

My Siamese cat's left a brown
snake, its back broken, on my desk.
The underground throbs outside my window.
The black highway of the river's crinkled by a light
westerly blowing down. I want to give praise
to the coming winter, but problems
of belief flare and buckle under
the lumpy syntax. The unelected
President's on the radio again,
laying waste to the world.

Faith—that old lie. I drag up
impossible meanings and double divisions
of love and betrayal, light and dark.
Where on earth am I after all these years?
A possum eats crusts on the verandah,
standing up on its hind legs.
My weakness can't be measured.
My head contains thousands of images—
slimy mackerel splashing about in the murk.
My failures slip through fingers pointed
at the best night of my life. This one.

The cold mist falls, my head floats in a stream
of thinking. Eurydice. Did I fumble? Maybe
I was meant to be the moon's reflection
and sing darkness like the nightjar. Why
wouldn't I infest this place, where the
sun shines on settlers and their heirs
and these heirlooms I weave
from their blond silk?

LOVE POEMS

∿

Shafts of light disintegrate into clues
flecked symbols shine with order

Sail Away

Our day was composed of resemblances. Take
the heavy cloudbank as a mountain, as it lifted
itself up from behind the headland: how

its appearance altered to disintegrating
fluxive streaks as we spoke. We were sitting quietly
by the river as the colours changed.

And as we spoke—however gingerly—we knew
the blackbird in our voice, and watched it flying
there, high above the water, until our

conversation resembled its elusive song—
though it was the bird that sang amidst the rolls
of thunder and, as we listened, its notes

rose and fell around us on the ridiculous earth,
so that all we really saw was in the sky
of that electric evening. Maybe it was summer

and it was summer's shifting colours
through which our blackbird tumbled, as if evening
was not an imagined time: so in the orange

atmosphere the blackbird darted from my voice
to yours, and we almost held each other by the hand.
A breeze ran along the surface as if it was

a breeze, and the surface of the river
kicked against it, as if there was a tide coming in.
The blackbird sang as if it had a song.

Harriet Westbrook
Looks at the Serpentine

We reached Edinburgh
and were alone
a few days together
from then it was always
some bitch, some poet
or another. The days
flowed into days,
nights like dark moths
fell about me. Your
dream of perfect love
betrayed us Bysshe
you took it not me
then blew us away, threw
my love in the air
and watched the wind
float it off like paper.
How many times I tried
folding it up, holding it
for sheets to write?
You'd use it for kites
to fly with our fights
in the Scottish weather.
Bleak days after
crazed nights; now there's
no God like you said,
no harbour to shine
brilliant with bright sail,
it's a black mud, a slimy
stream, fit place for
the Mad Woman of Queen St.

Your once radiant wife
is skipping out
with the dragon's tail—
though not for you, this
is mine, taking one
last lesson from your strife,
know with me Shelley, how to die.

Couplets

↝ for Juno

On days still when the tide's full, river
hours with you are momentary fire

in the head, shall not stay memories
even, so intensely lived: just to sense

bay calm and watch the seconds scatter.
These cupped hands of brackish water

evaporate as light fragments in hair flicker
with mangrove's shade for your skin—

I know grassbanks where we rolled together
on the shaggy cotton-brush, now remember

not to remember any day other than our
morning on Jerusalem Bay, there as tide

turned the stern, our boat was afloat on a mist
rolling in, full of the song of the wattlebird.

The Details Necessary

Tar on the dirt drifts to afternoon's
edges, slopes of winter, animals
and birds in the ground, trees—
the domed sky's early stars strung
to earth by tails of mist.
The full moon is translucent orange
and moves the far mountain
deeper into distance. I know words
will trouble my poem tonight
though I can't be bothered
with all that, anyway I'm sure
Susan Sontag is working on it,
somewhere in Greece or maybe
New York, sitting at her wicker table
facing some wall or window
full of intricate geometries—
or maybe she's given up reading books
again and just sits there,
her head rocking with the puzzle
of Artaud's Platonic imagery, who
knows—though she's sure
to be covering the problems of things
like this: writing poetry in '88
on the side of a river in Australia;
she'll be thinking about
the 'old questions,' dovetailing
them into the new. Tonight
I'll open my lines to love, desire—

desire for my wife, craving for a chance
to love her here, under
Hawkesbury moon, taking her
into our bedroom, turning out
the electricity, opening the window,
holding her until we shine with carnality,
dropping awhile the weight of poetry, art,
photography—though maybe using
them for loving until our bones are
liquid fire—our bodies given
to each other in postures
of alchemy and praise, as if we
were the gods we have relentlessly
tried to believe through others.
Here we would be new and know it as we
fondled our imaginations
through our bodies; I would take her
carefully and begin to kiss
from her toes slowly up into the little
wings of her cunt, her breasts
until their long nipples were full
in my mouth; our hands following
our hearts until our bodies arched over
the bed in colours our senses
would invent for the rest of our lives,
and live then the hours
in all the details that are necessary,
as complex as the language
Susan Sontag needs to use when
she shares with us her passion
and admiration for Artaud's mystic poems,
where flesh and thought are one,
where the day becomes the poem looking into
what must be done.

Songs for Juno

I

My lies are for you, take them utterly, along
with the truth we are explorers for.
An old skiff mutters, pushes up Hawkesbury mud—
the image comes in, drifts, sinks, disappears:
shape-changing gods, we dream in separate bodies;
a part of it, we want feathers for sails;
the rivers we dance stand upright in the sky,
distance between them—though at headlands
fork, touching mix, become ocean.

II

Wind and the sails full in dreaming with you.
We talk of great deserts, old chalk cities,
ice language and its lava. Then imagination darts,
Tasmania appears filling our bedroom, sails
are wings of geese, homing ocean, white tricks
of the distance. How do we leave our tiny pasts?
My love, time fragments, blows into space—
we ride, fly, sail in every way we find there is
to now. Bring us a new language, to remake
these questions, into dream, the gale, I whisper
to you softly.

III

How long in these secret places from childhood—
the old embers smoulder on, the lowlands
laced with fire-lines, long spokes turning
in sky—were we at play—or were the games more
half-remembered charms, songs? We inhabit,
are rocked by still those innocent passions.
Dressed up for the new ritual, we move
the circle more than dance it. Take the moment,
hold it to you, the new, my brave and frightened
lover is a sacramental kiss. Our dreams touch—
warm with light. Give me your nightmares too.

IV

Paint flaking from the belly of an old clinker.
The boys with their rods, prawns
and bloodworms rubbed through their hair,
tasting the westerly around Snake Island—
and you sleeping, curled around the stern.
The mountains everywhere, skirts of the mangroves,
then at Dangar's jetty, an octopus
sucking for its life at the end of a line.
Blue wrens hovering for invisible insects, a shag
hunched on a wing. The trim park
patched there amongst the scribbly gums,
houses, a wash-shed, and in a backyard
lemongrass drying in the sunlight.

V

The new list begins.

Clear Water Reckoning

I write into the long black morning,
out here on the end of the point,
far from my wife in Budapest—
as the river cuts through a mountain
in Sydney a poet is launching
his new volume *Under Berlin*
and I feel like Catullus on Rome's edge
but this passes and I turn to face
the oncoming dawn, the house
breathes tidal air as the night
fires outside with barking owls,
marsupials rustling, the prawn bird
beginning its taunting dawn whistle;
I burn the electricity
and measure hours by the lines—
I have strewn words around the living room,
taken them out from their
sentences, left them unused wherever
they fell; they are the bait—
I hunch over my desk and start to row,
let the tide flow in, watch
the window, with the door locked now
I wait—hear satin bowerbirds
scratching out the seeds from bottlebrush.

Dawn is a thin slit of illuminated
bowerbird blue along mountain lines,
in this year of cock and bull
celebration the TV goes on unwatched
upstairs, I hear it congratulating us
for making Australia what it is—
the heater breathes out a steady stream
of heated air—I go deeper
into my head, I see the Hawkesbury
flowing through Budapest, the Hungarians
do not seem to mind, they are bemused,
the river parts around their spires and domes,
I see other cities, whole cultures
drawn from territories within,
though with this freedom
comes a feeling of strange panic
for the real; so I get on
with it, writing out from this egg
holding my thought in a turbulent knot,
a bunched-up octopus. I steer
away from anything confessional,
thinking of Robert Lowell crafting
lines of intelligent blues,
his Jelly Roll of a self-caught mess
deep in spiritual distress.

Outside the river pulls me back,
shafts of light disintegrate into clues,
flecked symbols shine with order—
the bowerbirds have woven colour
around the house, through
bushes blue patterns of themselves
traced about the place; half
the moon can topple a mountain,
anything is possible here
I remind myself and begin to hum,
flattening out all the words that were
impossible to write today. I hum
out all the poems I should have
written, I hum away now also
the desire to write from memory—
there is enough sorrow in the present.
I look out over the incoming tide, dark racks
of oysters jut from its ink.

Full Tide

My whole being's the bay,
cradled in the warm palm
the steady open hand of today's
flood tide. Anyway
let's tell the fishermen
something they already know—
it's the fabled calm
before the flow: I love
a gypsy with a lithe
soul who's difficult to please.
So may the resonance
of this new psalm begin life
here, then moon-change
phase to phase—It's fishermen
who recognise my strength,
who say to keep an eye
on me, then look long
at her art, sense vision's
power—the dance,
intellect and body, her total
elegance. Ah river
with ageless dreams, sorceress
with sea-hawks and gliders,
up-drafts in phosphor-fire, eyes
quick for your lips, thighs—
speak, tell me fables
as you flow. Ah tide that stops
dead, for my wild Magyar—
genuflecting from your ancient bed.

The Channels

᠇ for Orlando

At Mooney there had been killing
from the start, from mudflat to creek—

in the name of the river spirits,
it was death to the fish: so the shores

are hallowed where we fought for your future
through silence on deep water.

Fierce heads breaking ancient tide
and I called blood, feathers and scale,

my boy, bones of the trees—
I had forgotten love until you

stood your ground, though it was a child's

and filled with the new laws of cities.
I was afraid for your senses

and soul; so here I'll twist phrases
to sing again the old lores

and say the love a father would—
there with your eyes filled with the shiny

life, your dreams of style, jets
and tropical adventures, you were a savage

pride with a high mind aflame.
I shook as I spoke you down, rocked

to the bone by your blunt tongue—
and I will again engage your temper

with the magic of language:
let me offer what I can as a hard man

softened by my becoming a father
to you, of your unknowable

future, questing and burning for more now,
that we go on always.

Fishing with My Stepson

We wake by your watch on my wrist,
its piercing silicon chip
alarm bat-squealing, needling
through our room in the Angler's Rest.
We drink Coke from a plastic Esky
with ice melting into newspaper
wrapped squid, the only
unfrozen bait in town. In perfect dawn
we set out from Don's Boats,
the outboard ploughs us through a bay,
at Juno Point we cast our silver
Tobys, our new Swedish lures.
Your pure graphite rod flashes
at first light—a graceful cast
sails out fine as a spiderweb,
the smooth water mirrors the arc.
A year passes in the minute it takes
for you to reel in your first true catch,
the rod-bending, line-singing
realising strike and the flash of fish-fire,
the final buck underwater dash
of a school of jewfish, its explosion in air,
and for that split second of communion
between us, utter wonder.

Flannel Flowers for Juno

We walk along a crumbling bush track,
the full moon dropping through gums,
down through the sparse limbs,
their shredded bark hanging by balance—
thinking in fragments.

The air's damp and sweet.

The sounds of the river are softened
while you carry the rest of the world in your head
and I empty myself of memories one
word at a time.

They sink behind us onto the floor of the bush.

Your face shines with competence,
your hair flows, I hold your warm hand as we walk.
It feels miraculously alive compared to my
dry mouthings.

Whatever we pass by seems very old.
Twigs petrified into black glass crack under our feet.
A tawny frogmouth owl looks at us from a dead branch
unblinking, immobile, eternal.

I can't ask you for forgiveness.
Words aren't part of this landscape.
The weight of what I've done grinds away at my knees,
the joints of my bones scrape away the word 'jelly.'
My head floats on the path beside you, its hair
speckled pollen from flowering gums.

You turn to gaze into a sandstone cave.
Above the entrance, flannel flowers
grow from the roots of an ancient fig,
their blossoms closed against the dark.

The First Chance Was the Last

Down sandstone steps to the jetty—always
the same water, lights scattered across tide.
Remember, we say, the first time.
Our eyes locked into endless permission,

this dark gift. Why can't I let go
and be the man in your life—not the one who writes
your name on the dedication page; whatever
the name, you know who I write for,

you know how private, how utterly selfish
these musings are. This is your image,
crafted in the long hours away. The house
rocks, money comes and goes, fish

jump against tide. The children grow
and go out into the world. The bleak eye
turns, my tongue speaks with ease—a rudder
steering the stream of words into their

daily meanings. I cried out when you weren't
here, I smashed my fist against stone. Art was stone.
A red glow cracked the kitchen window. I carved
the roast and served it to the cats.

Signposts point the way. Bitter laughter stings,
my black heart beats. This way to the shops
and gallery in the ordinary day. Clap your
hands against my ears, turn off the lights—

you stay. Is it always you? Shapes change,
music becomes a pool of melancholy sea-water
distilled in sun, slapping rock—a seagull's eye
reflecting a shoal of whitebait alive with death.

Love makes an art that walks in a son
and moves a daughter. We move
through time and sing in the light:
the first chance was the last.

Fishing in a Landscape for Love

This is swamp land, its mountains
worn down by the wings of kingfishers
flying back to their nests. Crows
are black feathers

saving me from morning.
I talk to them as if we're friends,
they look at me sideways.
When I offer them fish they eat it.

Swamp harriers whistle as they do
slow circles through the azure—
let's talk about the azure,
descriptions of place

can't imitate the legs of prawns
moving gently in the tide
from which the azure takes on meaning.
I put them into a mosquito-wire cage

and lower them from the jetty,
they jump from their sleep
at the dark of the moon.
Bait is all that matters here—

love's worn down into sound
and is contained in what I say,
these dead words feeding on live ones,
these ideas thrown to the crows—

they don't come back,
love needs live bait,
it doesn't behave
like a scavenger.

Brahminy Kite

Humidity envelops my boat, black mould
embellishes its trim. There are mullet-gut stains
on the seats. Tides flood in across the mudflats
and small black crabs play their fiddle-claw
with a feeble left bow, day in, night out.
My hand swoops to catch a lure.
Talons pierce scales and a heart.

We grasp the core only gradually
of each other's compressed midnights—
black roses flowering in sandy-eyed dawns,
memories stowed to starboard, where a
brahminy's wings catch first light.
How did we manage it, sailing
on—weathering

leagues of years? We're a far cry now from
beating wings and arched poetic myths:
the swell's escalator takes us up over the top
of the world into white crests and gull-squawk.
Now there are fields of light to relinquish
and dolphin fish skittering around
markers, slicing apart an oily sea.

Off Barrenjoey, the kite hits thermals,
then lifts into a triple rainbow stained with
yellowtail blood and slime. Its beaked head fits over
my face, sea-spray stings my eyes. In the haze
beyond tiredness, its wings cut through
an atmosphere thick with salt
and the glint of fish scales.

ON NOT SEEING
PAUL CÉZANNE

ح

Everything that matters comes together
slowly, the hard way, with the immense and tiny details,
all the infinite touches, put down onto nothing

Mondrian: Light Breaks upon the Grail

The skiff carelessly up against rocks
Oysters   cleaning the fish   mosquitos
on my thighs as I crouch in mangroves
silted roots force themselves

up into air   consciousness
seeks form here   shape these lines
in your mind   solids set down
church built from the local sandstone

by the river in a dark corner
where blessed shadows have crept back
and forth for a century or more
so far from Piet's white room

arranged to display human order
fish-knife sparkles in sunlight
tide-line junk shows even here
how they've smeared his pure contemplation

tobacco packet's lettering
red with heavy black rules—
Sun dries fish-blood on arms
shirt and the clockwork of fishing tackle

my skiff up against the rocks   climbing
through swamp mahogany trees
sharp air to brace wounded lungs
stumbling into dry bracken

my eyes lining things up
strange to seek form here
consciousness is its own place   too late
the red bottlebrush shakes with honey-eaters

Beyond the Pale

∽ for Tim Storrier

The certainty of it all, as clear as clear water,
like the sky a thousand miles out
into the desert, the complex distances
between horizon and sun. The expectation
of solitude, alive with reds
and the wild desert blues, with light
sinking into anything that stands upright.

On the way we notice coloured ensigns
emblazoned onto the windows
of the final service stations—winged horses,
golden rams, scallop shells; the night neon
pulsing through their skin.
I remember you saying something like:
'if a thing is made well enough,
it has a soul, the craft itself imparts
the craftsman's.' I looked again—the soul
of a glass scallop?—then marvelled
at your carpenter's trust for the next fifty miles.

On dawn the landscape we sailed through
became horizontal, we passed the ruined craft
of wrecked houses, destroyed fences
and random posts leaning at angles
into the gnarled scrub. We looked straight
ahead, in silence, wanting to talk,
though not of this desert junk. Is the stump
the indigenous art of this scene, pole,
post and pale—necessity? A totem
that can both dispel fear of the dark, night—
then by day embellish itself
with the refractions of sunlight passing through
the atmosphere.

Outside we noticed the convex distance
shimmering into sky, the road flying
into it, an Egyptian measuring ribbon.
Soon our reckoning and what we have
imagined will meet out here, at some
ground zero of time, beyond the shadow sticks
of palings—on a plateau of light
so brilliant not even tone could forge
its tricks with shape. Now earth rushes
on all sides, we take bearings from each other;
a half completed phrase, eyes sliding aside,
awkward gestures. The signs we make

signifying our ease with the interior life,
the privacy of art. We smell the motor labouring
on the invisible slope. Everything
that appears makes us think of permanence;
our heads imagining two flecks of onyx
moving across this waste of light.

Our campsite appears to vibrate
in the sunlight, we move under the canvas
shades and look out to the horizon. We create
signs then stake lives on them—signs
can't be constant in themselves, like tokens, chips
of black opal, flung into the sun's abyss.
There's no future other than oblivion
for our signs and their dogged followers.

I scratch some lines onto a rock with the chalky
femur of some perished marsupial—then confide
in you—'These are runes.' You turn calmly
and concur with, 'Then they are' …
and my head fills with dismay.
So the only permanence is in what we
say, what we imagine through language,
a permanence neither within nor beyond the pale.
The fine and burning line of art, the fence.

Drawn with Light

An owl swooping low over the city, silent
down through a lane, hooks a rat
then back to the glass tower, its roost—
    owl-eyes adrift, drawn by moonlight,
like winged cameras of modern seers
            fire glows in the fallacy of images
the passage of light. (In this age
  of ferocious mumbling, we are drawn
to the silent language)
            these are the images we live with.
Our bodies move across light, torn
    forms manipulated to tilt sight's edge
into darkness: Clever emblems
created for the conjuring advertiser,
            pornographic marks
politicians describe, their faces
                    across front pages—
Sport heroes, suspended in the air
    to sell alcohol, pictures of sleek yachts
their spinnakers ablaze
            with multicoloured jingoism.
Streets of homeless, suburbs of living dead,
  beaches alive with the young
and beautiful, missions of dispossessed—
                    images we live with
            And do we also prey upon them?
Owls of art, silent as images
        gliding through studio and gallery
over glossy pages, pruning our conscience
            fine-tuning aesthetics

Do we see the world we cannot see through art,
   use vision's virtue, particular
emotions creating sight—Drawn with light
         so that the image perfects itself
in our seeing it—Drawn out from dark to make
   bright images of life in our living it

lucidity, clear fire.

Rock Carving with Kevin Gilbert

The fish outlined on the rock
is the shape of a mulloway, we are moving
here under a fine yellow rain
pouring from the spear wound
in its side. A lyrebird dances above,
trembling the morning silk air.
We fish with two swamp harriers,
sweet whistling killers like us, who cut
fish throats and clasp up
bunches of silver nerves—
calling under stars convicts
hacked in the cliff face.
We crush oysters with rocks
and throw them as berley into the tide
we call our Milky Way.
After a while stingrays
come on the bite, then one after
another, brown-winged,
hump-backed, yellow-bellied
bull-rays fight to their death—
we cut some free to watch slide
over carvings of themselves,
back into the drink, as the rock mulloway
moves its shallowing grooves.

The Art Critic

Out here on the windy stream the lecturer
weathers his dream, his little boat
moored by a loquat tree shuffling its yellow
fruit. For months the papers have

hovered over his bed. Tonight he marks
them, on Fridays he writes his piece on art.
His boat is a mild addiction, a darker
side where he seeks atonement

for a fissure he hides. The shape
of a black mussel picked from a pylon:
he throws it into a pot then eats the flesh
of his small sin. If art can serve

a theory it will sing. When night comes,
the gorge out there will brim with mist.
He will cough wisps of it at dawn.
As he tries to gargle the song of a bullfinch

feathers will float out from the bristles
on his chin. In his head there's a mallet
he lets thud through his dreams, but after
the marking he will flower, and the students

won't even know. A newspaper hits a mat
on his verandah prickled with frost.
His piece is published. The sun will strike,
and the bullfinch sing through his fountain pen.

After Brett Whiteley

We're on this looping road, it's narrow
and the car's fast and expensive,
too fast considering we've downed a few.
There's a woman singing Bob Dylan well,

too well as the line about what you want
cuts through the climate control
mixing the smell of jonquils with hot
bodies. Things are looking dangerous.

Then suddenly the waters are before us,
the surface a black raw silk all ironed out
and drifting through a fishy light.
We are still in the car and quibbling

as a wild duck makes an evanescent wake
across the phosphorous tide. The woman turns
to Brett and says: is this decadence? No man,
he mutters, just reflected glory up shit creek.

Meshing Bends in the Light

Just under the surface
mullet roll in the current;
their pale bellies catch
the sunken light, the skin
of the river erupts
above purling. The sky
hangs over the boat a wall
of shuddering light
smudging the wings
of a whistling-kite,
mudflats glow
in the developing chemicals,
black crabs hold their
claws up into the light
of the enlarger, yabbies
ping in the drain. A westerly
howls through the
darkroom. The tide
is always working
at the base of the brain.
The turning moon is
up-ended, setting on the silver
gelatin page: a hook
stopped spinning in space.
Owls shuffle their silent wings
and dissolve in the fixer.
Shape words over what you see.

The river flows from your
eyes into the sink, bulrushes
hum with mosquitos
that speckle the print.
The last riverboat mail-run
scatters letters across
the surface, the ink
runs into the brackish tide.

Reading Georg Trakl

⚘ for Garry Shead

Lovers gaze at each other
radiant in the afternoon's dimness
arms resting gently over shoulders
eyes reflecting the amber light

Beyond the black outline of the bush
a thousand birds rustle in branches
Inside your grandmother lights the kerosene lamp
setting loose its shadows

Near the house heavy fruit drops softly
onto the uncut grass in the yard
A breeze blows out the lamp
as you turn from the map of your canvas

and listen to the surf rolling sand back
onto the beach at Bundeena
You stay up all night waiting for sunlight
and to watch as the lovers dissolve with dawn

David Aspden's Red Theme

Parrots have subverted it, the
red-capped lorikeets completely green—
one pulls its talons together
into a little arthritic bunch.

Mondrian painted Hitler's moustache
with red pigment and linseed oil.
Saint Paul must have been considering red
as he dipped his quill in Christ's wounds.

Red spots on a double-bar's head—
an ornithologist plucks
a feather, thereby furthering
a breeding project.

Red on the wattle of a silky cock
waking a small town, where fishermen market
the last of the swordfish. Sunlight on lumpy oceans
where albatross dive for red hooks.

Powder Hulk Bay

ↄ *for John Firth-Smith*

Blocks of sandstone suspended in air
above the roadway on Old Spit Bridge.
Hours painted black. Black-capped
terns catching chips in the park.

We talked for twenty summers thinking it
meant something: sand sticking to sweaty limbs,
rasping voices buffeting families on the beach,
children, streaks of cloud moving through

afternoon light. Sails flaring on the blue surface
of the bay—slabs of meaning. Each painting
holds one: friends gone, scratches of writing
remembering what we should have said.

A peppercorn tree by the harbour shakes
with cicadas making their throbbing note stick.
One day a great bull shark swam up
to the side of our boat, almost touching.

Sealice scabbed its gills, trailing
a shredded wire trace from a fishing line.
It kept shaking its head, rolling an eye
as if to take us in. We froze, held the oars tight

and still. Whatever we said rose up into
the currawong's melodic fluting. A wing's streak
of white is all that separates us from the dead.
Encased in a wave of cicada sound,

we were a hair's breadth away from live bait—
and the water the colour of paradise, an indigo
black with news.

On Not Seeing Paul Cézanne

I think of the waste, the long
years of not believing the
tongue pretending

in the midst of words
to speak, to keep walking
that bend in the road

I cursed myself for not having spoken

The blank sheets of air could have added

Words smudged out and revised with a colour

stroked instead of butting
coming to the shape by layers, stumbling
in from the corners and rubbing out the hard light

The countless fish flapping on boards
Have they just disappeared?
there's no way

back to the water to catch
again that possible
colour

Outside the window in the black night
mosquitos gather under floodlights on the pontoon
until the empty westerly blows

Everything that matters comes together
slowly, the hard way, with the immense and tiny details,
all the infinite touches, put down onto nothing—

each time we touch
it begins again, love quick brush strokes
building up the undergrowth from the air into what holds

CANTICLE FOR THE
BICENTENNIAL DEAD

ॐ

*Australia we sobbed through the paperbarks' songs
to birds and the gentle animals
and to the soft-stepping people of its river-banks*

Wild Colonial Boys

Musk ducks and the plump Wonga pigeon
were knocked from the sky
in blood sport, left to rot, then afterwards
in firelight were the games,
all various forms of gambling. In the mist
you'd hear knuckle-bones rattle
in their cotton pockets or, darned
in conversation, obscene words, slurred
by badly brewed alcohol; never song
but garbled recitations, coughed half-chants.
Whatever fed the imagination
was like a yellowness: it showed
in various activities, from plucking
ducks to the way they slept in postures
of loose decadence. The river
was a flood of their refuse, a smear of thick
waste through the countryside. After
storms and at low tide you'd see the details
of their hate: the score, a tally and what they called
their stake—the sacred remnants
of an ancient tribe's estate.

Canticle for the Bicentennial Dead

They are talking, in their cedar-benched rooms
on French-polished chairs, and they talk
in reasonable tones, in the great stone buildings
they are talking firmly, in the half-light
and they mention at times the drinking of alcohol,
the sweet blood-coloured wine the young drink,
the beer they share in the riverless river-beds
and the back-streets, and in the main street—
in government-coloured parks, drinking
the sweet blood in recreation patches, campsites.
They talk, the clean-handed ones, as they gather
strange facts; and as they talk
collecting words, they sweat under nylon wigs.
Men in blue uniforms are finding the bodies,
the uniforms are finding the dead: young hunters
who have lost their hunting, singers who
would sing of fish are now found hung—
crumpled in night-rags in the public's corners;
discovered there broken, lit by stripes
of regulated sunlight beneath the whispering
rolling cell window bars. Their bodies
found in postures of human-shaped effigies,
hunched in the dank sour urinated atmosphere
near the bed-board, beside cracked lavatory bowls,
slumped on the thousand grooved, fingernailed walls
of your local police station's cell—
bodies of the street's larrikin Koories
suspended above concrete in the phenyl-thick air.

Meanwhile outside, the count continues: on radio,
on TV, the news—the faces
of mothers torn across the screens—
and the poets write no elegies, our artists
cannot describe their grief, though
the clean-handed ones paginate dossiers
and court reporters' hands move over the papers.

Silva

It came into being from the splintered limbs
swam out and flowered into being

from chopped saplings and wood-chips
its pages glowing and telling their numbers

this a numbat's fragile skeleton
this the imprint of the last chalk-moth

Members of court in the old languages
mumbled as wings of ground parrots flicked

At night we discovered new seeds
in an old gum's stump as shoals of insect memory

floated out from a bee-eater's nest
then the rasping call of an adder

We looked into the white-rimmed eyes of the elders
and wanted to turn away

until pages began stroking air
that carried back doves from the black bamboo

Australia the goshawk circled a lake
we croaked amphibian prayers to reflected skies

then stumbled off through the spinifex

Mornings threaded the whale bones with flame
as poetry baked like a rock

on the final page of dense black marble
of slate-thought that shone

until the eyes of a hunstman took us
into morning's spokes a white trap-work

where caught finches hung their hearts drumming

Australia we sobbed through the paperbarks' songs
to birds and the gentle animals

and to the soft-stepping people of its riverbanks

The Trophy

At the mouth of the estuary, a harbour-side
tourist town, the afternoon
is gold, the tide's in—twin Volvos
churn the shallows, the sleek
Pandora flies an ensign that signifies a kill.
At the wharf men haul
a blue marlin from the stern,
longer than a skiff, thick as an Arab stallion.
Its skin flares like molten emerald
in the sun; the sword-head
cuts through the picnic atmosphere—
the eyes are the size of a fisherman's fist,
the torn sail of its back flaps
on fiberglass, a leathery broken eagle,
the tail's a sickle.
The crowd moves over the wharf, gathers
around this beautiful animal,
some poke at the colossal death
until a man cuts the belly open, then in acid
some fish, a squid and mangled seagull
sludge into the air. The stench
scatters the crowd and a boy convulses on sand.
The man who made the kill now stands
posed by the hanging marlin with his son
being photographed.

Phasing out the Mangroves

Now it has been drawn up and swamp
will be filled, measurements
have been taken; now come perspectives,
balsa-wood models grow out
from colour-photography. It was life
say the eyes of the elderly;
replaced by concrete geometry—
The great hunched mangroves
will no longer tend
the instincts of kingfishers;
bent glass and metal domes shall hover
above mud that fed soldier-crabs.
Windsurfers will be flightless pelicans
and clouds of sandflies will rise
around neon-calligraphy,
where old wood knocks on jetties
will be echoes of graphite
and tending the keyboards on decks
of the river-craft, the swamp children
speaking a language of arithmetic in cracked syllables.

Remembering Posts

for Manfred Jurgensen

In this country, beyond the sparkle
and the junk, the weekend blood
arenas, beaches full of paddlepops
and shit, out along the road
you stop noticing flags for hamburgers
or the empire, it all becomes a streak
of colour smearing the windscreen—
as you drift freeways or swerve
and loop down narrow passes you
realise you could be anywhere
in the world in your head, though
nowhere else you'd feel like this—
a passenger of memory floating out
across centuries. After distance
lulls you become a mobile antenna,
taking it in as each nerve flicks
with pain, sensing flesh wounds
in the open-cut mountainside, broken
bones under desert crust. Now you
know that if you stop you would shoot
roots and grow branches, leaves,
flowers—or you'd spear yourself
into the earth and sprout up
like a telegraph pole, a grey post
on the edge of a gibber plain, and be
stuck there swaying in the dry wind,
remembering.

The Greenshank

Miklós Radnóti, marched from forced labour
in Yugoslavia back into Hungary, came to rest
near a bend in the Rádca, at what his translator
describes as 'a strange lonely place' where

the tributary joins 'the great river,' a marshland
watched over by willows and 'high circling birds.'
Condors perhaps—they appear in the notes and
poems he was writing—under a foamy sky.

Huddled in a trench with the body of a friend
who'd been shot in the neck, he wrote with a pencil
stub in his notebook: *patience flowers into death*.
His wife's face bloomed in his head.

Thinking of the petals of crushed flowers
floating in a wake of perfume, he wrote to caress her
neck. The fascists' bullets wipe out his patience.
His written petals survive.

Today, we listen to the news of war
here in a river sanctuary my wife's unbending
will has created—horizontal slats of cedar, verticals
of glass—a Mondrian chapel of light.

This afternoon just before dark the first
greenshank arrived from the Hebrides.
Ignorant of human borders, its migration
technology is simple: feathers

and fish-fuel, cryptic colour and homing
instinct. This elegant wader landed on a mooring,
got ruffled in the westerly, then took off again,
an acrobatic twister, and levelled down

onto a mudflat—a lone figure that dashed across
the shore, stood on one leg, then, conducting
its song with its bill, came forward
in a high-stepping dance.

Easter Fish

Tonight in the bright void of our kitchen, my wife
and her mother cooked dinner and talked of brutal places
at the end of the world and meals scraped together

from remnants: thin brown potato skins, tart green
bean soup. We discussed the rituals of Passover.
Charcoal lines from a recent bushfire cross-hatched

the trunks of ghost gums. Outside our kitchen windows,
a butcher bird appeared on the verandah, strutting
the rail and capriciously fluting.

Later our conversation filled an elegant apartment
in Budapest with music. We spoke—carefully, tenderly
perhaps—of the river, the unbroken Danube.

Our minds can flower suddenly sometimes
with monstrous kelp waving in the tide
flowing from old wounds:

brace yourself, cities of the world, against flood,
famine, invasion. Ruin. Now the river's surface
is stretched tight, marbled by a sun setting

in heads indwelling in silence. Puncturing the sky
upstream, a pair of sea-eagles spiral down to their nest.
We steamed our Good Friday fish,

seasoned with sweet basil and the juice of lemons,
and deliciously the taste brought back memories of its
capture: the mauve and silver flanks fading

into a quick death, the small cold flames of phosphorous
lapping our boat's invisible Plimsoll line, the rising
and falling of our breath.

The Flag-tailed Bird of Paradise

*(George W. Bush instructed 'the enemy' to hold up white
flags and stand twenty metres away from their tanks,
promising that if they did, they would be spared.)*

Thought to be extinct, they are appearing
through the red mist, their white tails
waving at blunt helicopters
splattering the earth. These creatures
from paradise play dead when attacked:
they freeze, clamped to a branch, the tiny
flags on their tails barely shimmering in
broken sunlight. They once lived
in jungles on islands in the Pacific,
but haven't been found dead there
since 1958. Some escaped to Arabia:
sold to collectors and bred in captivity,
they were taken up by zoos, kept in palaces
and inbred. Flunkies fed them and sultans
hovered about them, marvelling at how
they became extraordinary in their
deformities—their cream-coloured plumage
shot through with pale, beautiful rainbows,
their eyes enormous, pink, and their
flag-tails heavy—almost too heavy
to hold up, but not theirs
to withhold.

The Goldfinches of Baghdad

These finches are kept in gold cages
or boxes covered in wire mesh;
they are used by falcon trainers as lures,
and rich patriarchs choose these living ornaments
to sing to them on their deathbeds. Their song is pure
and melodious. A goldfinch with a slashed throat
was the subject of a masterpiece painted in the
sixteenth century on the back of a highly
polished mother-of-pearl shell—it burns
tonight in Baghdad, along with the living,
caged birds. Flesh and feathers, hands
and wings. Sirens wail, but the tongues
of poets and the beaks of goldfinches burn.
Those who cannot speak burn along with the
articulate—creatures oblivious to prayer burn
along with those who lament to their god.
Falcons on the silver chains, the children
of the falcon trainer, smother in the smoke
of burning feathers and human flesh.
We sing or die, singing death
as our songs feed the flames.

SWIMMING OUT WITH
EMMYLOU HARRIS

ॐ

The shining incidents, the language of oysters
and Hawkesbury River visitations

The Language of Oysters

Charles Olson sat back in his oyster-shed
working with words— 'mostly in a great
sweat of being, seeking to bind in speed'—

looked at his sheaf of pages, each word
an oyster, culled from the fattening grounds
of talk. They were nurtured from day one,

from the spat-fields to their shucking,
words, oysters plump with life. On Mooney Creek
the men stalk the tides for corruption.

They spend nights in tin shacks
that open at dawn onto our great brown river.
On the right tide they ride out

into the light in their punts, battered slabs
of aluminium with hundred-horse Yamahas on the stern
hammering tightly away, padded by hi-tech—

sucking mud into the cooling systems,
the motors leave a jet of hot piss in their wakes.
These power-heads indicate

the quality of the morning's hum.
The new boys don't wake from dreams
where clinkers crack, where mud sucks them under,

their grandfather's hands fumbling
accurately, loosening the knots. Back
at the bunker the hessian sacks are packed ready

and the shells grow into sliding white foothills.
A freezing mist clenches your fingers,
the brown stream now cold as fire:

plunge in and wash away last night's grog,
in the middle morning, stinging and wanting
the week to fold away until payday.

On the bank, spur-winged plovers stroll in pairs,
their beak-wattle chipped by frost,
each day blinking at the crack of sun.

Stalking for corruption? Signs.
Blue algae drifts through your brother's dream
of Gold Coasts, golf courses. The first settlement.

Farming the Oysters

They move their black stick bundles
across the river, put stakes
aside for fresh water, making racks
to drench in tar; oyster-farmers
who strive for an order
of their own, gardening their shells
bunching up smoked mullet
assorting old bleached branches
along a ragged shore—
on the stern-end of their punts
they stand. Staring straight ahead,
solitary figures, they power
along, driven by 100-horse Mercs
burning up and down the river,
blind drunk through dangerous
light; they bore towards shacks
tucked in the upper reaches,
proud-looking gentlemen in black
contemplating the stern's metal music.

A New Legend

In a friendless time the mind swims
out from its body: you become
all the lives you have ever lived.
In this clearing there have
been camp fires, though the ashes
are stone cold now. And the mist
just above the earth is
undisturbed. A brown kestrel flits

between the sun and the ancient
dwellings, its shadow a moth
wandering below the mist's surface.
Everything has been like this
for centuries. Sunlight struggles
through onto the petrified
branches of charcoal; as I walk
I create a new legend here—

my voice moves over the rock carvings,
my hands net for the moth's
faint dancing shadow, my eyes
vanish into the back of my head
and a small creature stops running.
The water lies still in granite
waiting for the chance to sing anew;
under the mist I become

a thousand echoes, sounding for
the time being. Wherever life emanates
it's born from my careful presence
here, treading: mushrooms bloom
in my footsteps among the ashes.
The mind moves ahead of my
body now, feeling the new wings,
wondering if they existed before.

Its thoughts lift me above the ground.
I look down at my body, a feeble
creature moving through its own silence.
Moss clings to my thighs, the kestrel
dives into the clearing hooking
up the creature I taught not to fear.

Drifting through Silence

Again she returns to me, in grey
morning, a complete woman.
The swamp is merely breaking in
her memory of another life: once
more her warmth rushes along
the filaments of my spirit. God,
where on earth are we travelling?
Huge wings unfold against

the earth, a breeze ruffles our
feathers as we move now
like native companions: the arrogant
brolga leaps amongst old stumps
of mangrove branches. When we
learnt to fly, we danced wildly in
the shadow of a new tree. Her
blood goes pulsing through tiny

constellations in my eyes: logic
says, impossible, impossible!
The bird leads us on, our planet's
drifting through silence without an
atmosphere of its own: we are
creating humming auroras, damp fern
grows up from the desert. Our
hearts beat of their own accord,

the stars come out from their pale
reflections, circling our heads,
I watch massive mangrove swamps rise
above the earth, the sun slowly
drying sap from their roots—a clear
river runs through the sky, empty
shells sing like kingfishers.
A new butterfly sails through a rain

storm—My love's voice sets out
for the throat of the nearest bird—
I call for more singing, she
sings less. An extinct night parrot
calls; we hear fugues impossible to
perform sound under dead water.

The Night Parrots

A song rose from thickets, your
song, continuing beyond warbling
catbirds. I had nothing to do
with it, wilderness came hurtling
toward me and I backed off, standing
still as a redwood with fear.
All my feelings rushed away, love
joined the skeletons of gentle

night parrots. A slovenly explorer
broke through swamps, terrified—
shooting wild animals, even though
his supplies were holding out.
He didn't bother eating the game;
the timid numbats were knocked into
undergrowth, bullets between
their eyes. Shale flaked from a

mountainside turning to grey sands,
I heard the sound of my love on the
verge of starvation: her song
spent on marsh water. She came for
my love that had turned to bone,
I simply watched. A mangrove tree,
centuries old, grew out from her heart,
its roots twining through her

body, feeding on her feeble spirit—
My mind rose above it all, observing
this from a distance. She wandered
into a swamp and slept on dead waters;
prawns began feeding on her undersides—
silence carried her spirit to the
tiny body of a kingfisher. King tides
flooded the swamp, covering

the whole myth with shining blue water.
The explorer struggles onto a shore
of grey sands, his men blasting away
at the shadows of teal and the spirits
of geese. He finally breaks camp,
under the skeletons of night parrots.

The Ghost Crabs

I flow back into myself with tide.
O moon that draws us and drives
us and we move through until we are
dancing. Balancing starlight on
the marshes, shaking the leaves
or calming the water. Feeling warmth,
ghost crabs come out, their claws
snapping held high in the air.

The river pulls at mangrove roots
as the ebb begins: standing to
my waist in water, prawns kick up
from under my toes—My love
would have me go now—moving off
with the river, skidding along
beneath the silt, head filled with
water. Now flexing my limbs,

the shock of feeling comes back
to my nerves: memories play
their part again. Swamp flowers are
opening, ready for sunlight,
vines twine closer to their branches
and a kingfisher ruffles its feathers
against the dew. She beckons from
the far shore, a chill runs

along my arms—I wade into shallows
calling, and straining my sight.
She moves there through the mist,
dancing and calling softly, hardly
moving the vegetation. My hands
shoot out over the tide, gleaming as
fish in a soft light. The senses
strain forward towards claws

turning and growing from the dawn.
I cannot reach, hands drift
down through the moonlight onto the
outgoing tide. Morning surrounds
me silently, sun hitting driftwood,
dead roots and branches.

The Speaking Page

When the tide moves again
   comes up over
      the point here
and spills
   into Parsley Bay,
     goes over
the river's torn entrails—
   your breath becomes
      tidal
atmosphere,
    it heals deeply
        thoroughly
   then you
begin to understand
      that the river
  is like a blank page
   your enter it
     differently: shape
 it as you would
   a new thought
      first vaguely
with phrases
   then sentences
     until finally
its language
   starts talking—
     when the river

covers a bay
　　you know its weight
　　　　soothes
healing the savaged earth
　　and the tide
　　　　begins to make music
as it covers oysters
　as it climbs
　　　　over the rocks
its song fills the valley:
　　a baroque
　　　　tinkling tune
　its lyrics
　in a language
　　　　easy to comprehend
of course
　　　its imagination
　　　　weaving
the river-song, your mind's
　　invention
　　　　is playing you
as the tide begins
　　to ebb
　and you see smooth mud
cuts healing
　　and there is wind-song
to dance now
　with your voice.

Landscape

The grey wharf creaks under
my weight, it's maybe
a hundred years since
the piles were sunk
and planks hammered down.
The river moves slowly
over mudbanks
swallows dive and glide
through clouds
of white ants in the low sky.
I take my fishing rod
shift weight onto one leg
and cast the bait out
in a long and graceful arc.
It splashes beside an old snag.
I look across the river
at a derelict house
its for-sale sign askew
on the paling fence—
in the backyard a bush
of rusted wire beside the great hulk
of a wrecked Chevrolet.

Folk Song

∿ for Kevin Hart

We live here by this
sliding water, brown by day
black at night

flecked with bats
and the blue powdery stars.
Morning, a kingfisher

sits, an indigo rock
knife-shaped, winking
sun-speckled. There are too

many of us here,
still they keep coming,
rockets and landmines pock

their dreams. Here
the long-billed ibis go savage
in the mangroves:

Egyptians, blown in
on some cosmic whim, they
plunge their heads

into the black mud swamp
and drag out long bloodworms;
the royal spoonbills

shake their crowns,
head feathers white calligraphy
of surrender. We sing

of the mulloway, our
mauve-scaled river cod. They
rise breaking the surface,

our songs mention
mulloway kills and at night
we eat the rich cream-coloured flesh.

Side of the Creek

Slender gums, flowering spray,
heliotropes at Bobbin Head.
The river calm, smoking.
Each day mangroves die off
a little more, though
their roots shoot upwards
from mud into the sweet air.
A kingfisher lifts up
a cat's eye in its beak,
nearby some fishermen
who do not laugh. At a toll
gate to the national park
a ranger sits in a glass box
drinking his cup of tea;
kingfisher wings sail
through his eyes in an amber
sea of whisky. Out on
the glassy river,
a battered oyster barge
goes purring by. One morning
a mangrove left a drop
of its blood on my
window-pane; the tree ferns
live through bushfires
and massacres, feeding
on time. I caught a tiny egg
as it fell from its branch
and placed it between
my wife's breasts; after a while
a blue chick hatched.

A koel tore the silence apart
with its double wolf-whistle;
the next night, looking
down through moonlight
onto the ebb, two huge black
water rats swam off, heading for town.

Ambivalence

Winter afternoon
an hour before

low tide,
two fishermen

are meshing
for the mullet

they net all
the way around

an oyster lease.
One coughs

his death rattle
drifts across

the flat dark
surface. The light

fades and they
bash the bottom

of their boat
with an oar

and a wooden club,
thud, thud, cough

cough. I watch
the mullet

boil under corks
of their mesh net,

great fish-rings
run slowly

over the tide,
serifs of death.

Swimming out with Emmylou Harris

A long curved horizon, the hazel coloured
tide and Lion Island
going by. A CD player skips
on the line. A quarter moon

in a ten cent town, on the swell
our wake shatters the reflection
of the real moon. We cut
through the sound of swimming,

the meaningless joy of living,
the random punishment of birth.
The song says, we all live up to what
we get—out here you believe

whoever writes the script.
Yesterday is reflected back by the moon;
mothers wash the sickly
smell from a dozen ruined shirts

every Saturday afternoon. Wives
turn their heads. There's an old grey
stingray spread-eagled across
the front of the chicken run,

three crows hop around it, the breeze
ruffling their satin collars.
They plunge their black beaks
into the lukewarm flesh. Emmylou,

your sweet holy music drifts
through the new curtains,
your song folds itself around the shack
filling the backyard, flowing through

our days, out on the back verandah
where Old Dutch sits slumped two days
into his latest coma. Sweet Lord,
sweet poison, sweet, sweet music.

A Visitation

All night, wildfire burned in the tree-tops
on the other side of the river. Now it's morning.
Smoking embers from the angophoras
are landing on the near shore
as a yellow-footed rock wallaby limps, dazed,
from the scrub, its fur matted,
its tail barely able to support its weight.
Although wounded, it seems miraculous:
the soft yellow of its feet, the hard, sharp black
of its claws. It's the first yellow-footer
I've seen for more than forty years. It takes
me back immediately to the time I was a kid,
rowing my grandfather's tallow-wood skiff across
Big Bay: I spotted a mob of four rock wallabies
that stood there as I sat silently in the boat
and let the tide carry me right by them.
One, I noticed, seemed to have mange—
it had mottled fur on its back—like the river foxes
in those days. Then a panic ran through
them: the largest buck bounded, almost flew,
straight up an enormous rock; the sheer wildness
and ferocity of it shocked me. Afterwards,
the atmosphere was thick with an odour unlike
anything I recognised. This morning, it's in the air
again. I turn to take another look, but the
rock wallaby's gone.

ELEGIES

۶

*Two hundred years ago the dictator Creon said to Antigone
who was the daughter of Oedipus and Jocasta:
'Go to the dead and love them.'* —SUSAN HOWE

Sonnets for Robert Duncan

1

Life today is a flowering bush of blue,
the windy harbour's alive with light,
red sun turns city glass to sheets of silk.
It's afternoon, the reflections caught

by translucent bays marble edges of the view—
bitter news is distilled by polite talk,
death has arrived again, hearing of it
shears from memory images of Francis Webb,

another poet who sang words into thought,
made phrases abstract for a figurative God.
Now Duncan's death succeeds more

than most, his life opened days, brought
song to nights where silence riddled prayer.
It isn't enough to weave more silk

2

the rhetoric's a holy gibberish, and cocoons
have fallen to their hungry worms
before they're even spun: I have only
a dumb reaper and Duncan's hand-woven psalms,

only the poetry. Only his words
and for all his talk of angels, they become
also creatures of the language we spoke in.
I imagine his consternation with 'only'

Only the poem! I hear the strict tone
in reprimand, music of anger composing itself,
though now impossibly. Here I point

to his death, still even surrounded by it—
pouring from heaven or rising from the stench,
only the poem, though be compelled begin another.

3

Make this death's loom, take up the lyre
strung to play rhymes pulled taut across
slangy syntax, something of calm awareness
in song, a finality grows from loss—

What *does* the Worm work in its cocoon?
Do I finally understand this arcane question?
revealing the silken vanity of talk
with death—though why reprimand a tone

of voice when it's the content
breaking the news—as now the red sun
is being eaten on a glass building-side

by a flashing neon sign spelling out
black homilies and jingles for the State:
have safe sex and spoil the Reaper's fun.

4

Now shred all irony to ribbons and trail
them from a ferry leaving Kirribilli wharf
in memory of Frank Webb—he sailed
there with his grandfather and walked

by the coal freighters where he'd meditate—
he called himself a pirate of peace
as he traced with his fingers a carved shark
that sanctified the rock. It is a place

poets have sung for centuries, so I take
a bearing here for Duncan, amidst languages
that shape this bay into a face—

though whose? Whoever's god now assuages
the harbourside with songs we can belong to,
life-torn words for death's menagerie.

No River, No Death

I

Awake after years: sudden exploding mangroves
alight as Mooney vanishes in mountain shade—

late afternoon, confusion of words, language
alive with a life of its own, lashing

out then licking its flesh wounds.
Words of the river, swarming in branches

of mangrove with prawn birds and fruit bats
and mullet butting upstream,

schooling, leaping,
and bull-nosed singing mullet songs—

silver green needs being spun till the spawn is done.

The river hawks tear at the heart's flesh, eat,
love to fly, in a moment's pocket of heaved air

where they are mullet's fear. Though here
on the tide's line, a torn wing of stingray

waves in wash, prawns fester on the underside.

2

Now leave from a jetty, souls going where souls go.
The world's a mudbank in a dank westerly

and there's nothing to hand, nothing to hold,
death's all around in the afternoon air.

Here with the spirits of river gods, the lost,
lost in a holy place, its histories

entangled with sadness, deep sorrow's
in the rotting and remembering.

Over this: planks, cut from swamp, return—
hewn from trunks in their green years

now creaking complainers in the dull sun.

The wharf sags with tar-drenched oyster racks
and a fisherman's punt rocks at its side for Charon.

3

Nets circle the mullet school, the fishermen
shake their mesh and the old rope stings

the stumped fingers and crooked thumbs,
then the fish buck under and die

in the net's wing-lock; like a cloak cast
out from the fishers' minds the green tide's

gone black and the mullet are done,
hauled to their death from the spawning run.

4

Now here in a creek on Mooney Bay all river
life calms the head that broods

on politicians oceans away, microwaved
down to our side of the planet,

their sickness infecting the silt of this tide.
They are death men rattling loaded dice,

war-headed malformations of the mind
as an eyeless reaper, its cloak space-fabric,

its titanium blade, its skull powdering radium,
with the crippling power of crab-thought

turning its claws onto its own black flesh.

To feel it here with the ancient river
alive in a crawling

flying prehistoric line drawn on a rock—
here in the belly of the serpent's beginnings—

is to know we may not go where all souls go.

5

We live with the threat of that white flash
until again like hawks we gamble

with flesh, with oblivion—

and tear from the thin blue wind the black heart
of the cave our sick heads come from.

6

The afternoon's last light has gone under now.
A flying fox swims in through a star,

catfish are pecking the stingray's wing.
The larrikin prawn bird starts to sing.

Creon's Dream

The old hull's spine shoots out of the mudflat,
a black crooked finger pointing back to the house.
On the dead low the smell of the mangroves.

The river seeps through the window, the books
are opened out on the desk. When the first breeze
hits the curtain the cats scatter.

It could be dawn for all I know, concentration
wanders through Creon's words to Antigone
Go to the dead and love them—okay so they live as

long as I do—what else can I make of it?
The bright feathers from a crimson rosella lie
in clumps on the floor with a pair of broken wings.

In the dark I try to write and remember the zoo
I played in as a child. There was a balding sedated lion
and a wedge-tailed eagle hunched on a dead

tree in a cage; they threw it dead rabbits
in 1953. The whooping cranes sidestepped
the concrete ponds and whooped all night.

The blue heron flaps across the river in my head,
poddy mullet hanging from its tight beak.
Ah, dead fish, the old black crow, the sick pelican.

I pad the room, out there mangroves are pumping up
the putrid air, life goes on. At the zoo they
still throw the animals dead meat, the big cats

are bred in labs where they lock the albino
freaks away. I pace the kitchen: where are the books,
who reads the poems? I take a drink, ribbonfish

swim across my pages, I shake my head but they swim on—
in low flocks, chromium ribbons, they fly under
the river herding up the poddy mullet,

rippling the surface, as the tawny frogmouth knows.
The books have gone, the spoonbills wade in
with whitebait skipping ahead of them,

channel-billed cuckoo come swooping after the crows,
flying low over the water, calling their mates,
dipping their hooked beaks into the moving chrome.

I sleep in broken snatches and dream nothing.
Mosquitos suck at my cheeks and empty bottles
clutter the verandah, the books are in darkness

but the sandy whimbrels finger the pages, words
dissolve, waves of the dead arrive in dreams.
Out there the black finger points to the mouth

of the river, where the dead are heading, they
move over the window glass. The extinct fins move
the fingers of my grandfather, mending nets,

the dead friends sing from invisible books. The heron
picks the blood-shot eyes from my father's terrible
work in the kilns and the darkness is complete.

Cornflowers

❧ *In memoriam Robert Harris*

In a skiff, anchored
on the edge of a mangrove
swamp, he gave me

a version,
an unpolished song,
something that might have

gone unspoken
in our bright lives;
there is no dark side

he told me: things
will glow, sing or die though
if we want them to,

it's all alive,
I just want to know who
owns the conversation

we may have some day, who
owns the dialogue
he repeated as

a flathead slapped
and shuddered
in the belly of the boat,

its pale speckles
flaring, the blue
barred tail fanning air,

who owns the words
as they hovered
with plump mosquitos

and collided with
a whiting in flight
down a cadence of dancing

particles, our
hearts locked in their
cages of singing muscle;

it was concerning
this theme, he continued,
that I composed a tune

for the cornflowers
to sing, cut, sitting
on my table in an indigo jar.

Elegy from Balmoral Beach

for Arkie Deya Whiteley

A beach. Small waves and a shark net.
Moonlight on a fig tree, the bay a black mirror.

Music coming from a house, an exquisite guitar.
Tonight, there's nothing more bitter.

Resonating chords float above the school yard,
night birds beat the humid air. The ebb tide

exposes the moon's haul: squabbling seagulls
slicing open the body of a drowned rat.

A light flickers, a newspaper floats. Doc Watson's
playing sounds like a waterfall, almost gentle.

Tonight the harbour's incandescent.
You arrive in an empty boat.

IN THE NIGHT

ℭ

Towards abstraction and darkness—poems of doubt,
memory and what I have of faith

Goshawk over Broken Bay

Pale morning through mist settles on the bay
And lifts a hawk into the chilly air.
Warm inside my house I lean back on a chair,
Gaze through frosty windows at mid-winter's grey.

A lone fisherman walks the rocky shore.
The hawk hovers, white, on a breeze above the beach:
Winter ghost-wings, out beyond my reach.
I check a field guide as sunlight moves over the floor

And meets the grate of my electric fire.
The man and bird are fishing from the headland's reef:
Seen through glass, distortions of my grief
Kindle the flames of a theatrical desire.

The hawk tumbles for its balance in a pocket of air.
I hold the bird book tightly in my hands.
My whole life seems curbed by these demands
For order—I fling back the chair,

Stride straight through the back door to the high
Verandah and stare directly at the hawk.
There is no order: just excuses for more talk.
I turn, instead of jumping from the rail I sigh.

Toward Abstraction / Possibly a Gull's Wing

The most disconcerting feature is an absolute flatness
especially the sand. I've been here in love
and having passed the perfectly calm ocean had only
noticed the terns—If there was some way
back, some winding track to follow I'd possibly find
the elusive agents of creativity.

As now for instance, I am completely indifferent
to the sad way that fellow moves over the sand ... Who?
Let's be pure in observation, let's drop opinions—
Look: he stops and, throwing off his towel,
runs into the surf, where stroking out he attracts the terns
that begin to curve above him.

Now look back to the beach. It is mid-winter.
The sand's deserted and eddies of windcaught grit are left
to dance and fall unhindered. At the far end of the beach
is an object—a rifle, rusting. He comes out from
the surf, stubbing his toes, heading towards the place
where the rifle lies melting.

The sand whispers beneath his feet as he passes by the gun.
Dazed, he goes in no particular direction.
The surf rolls a dead tern onto the sand and he kicks it.
Its wings unfold like a fan, sea lice fall from the sepia
feathers and the feathers take flight.

Rimbaud Having a Bath

To have been held down in a park
the animal breath on your face
hands tightening on the throat
grappling at you in the dark

A life lashing out to embrace
the flesh and green bones under it
and then the infected slime
injected by the half-erect cock

Remains a flesh wound until
morning and poetry begin their work
in the carnage under the skull
The great poet goes home again

to his mother and becomes
the boy he is and feels the pain
subside his senses numbed
by the fire boiling the water
and the yellow soap in the copper

He takes a rag and pumice stone
and slides his naked body in
Because he has taken this bath
he has betrayed his art having washed
the vermin from the body and the heart

The Home, The Spare Room

I am the poet of the spare room
the man who lives here

with television's
incessant coloured noise

between the ads keeping the children
at bay

At night I walk the seagrass
down the hall

my head rolls before me
like some kind of a round dice

which room tonight?

I think of my wife-to-be
who has thrown herself down

in a foetal shape onto her bed

I am a hard man, a vicious seer
who simply wants

to go on living—love is beyond me

if it exists—my heart,
so called, is as efficient as a bull's

and as desperate
for the earth's treasures—

I turn into the spare room
and begin to write a poem of infinite

tenderness

In the Night

The sheets are wrapped about me
I wake in a bad mood
you stand in the centre of it
It's been four days since I was with you
now you enter my dreams
in the same mood as I left you
petulant your head in
some old tantrum
I untangle myself and get up
then walk out into the dark house
my feet pad the cold
once again I hear the empty words
repeating promises vows a pledge
impossible charms against age and despair
We have all our lives left to live through
why must we watch ourselves
here in the present repeating our
selves our love hopeless
we hack away at our heads
our faces tense rubbing in the salt
our skin drawn the top lips
hanging loose
We have made the rendezvous
though each time we meet and touch
is another wound that will not heal

Why do we insist on being
real this way there is
a life each day the colours
surround us and at night we work
or sleep between television
and the bright moments of solitude
strange dreams of courage
I reach the kitchen moonlight
the smell of cooked meat
the luminous circle of the stove-clock
I turn and go back into
the living room
my family is sleeping I sit at my desk
and stare at the blue machine
In your house across the harbour
you wake turn on your side and curse me
Okay call me a ghost of a man

Into Forest

My face the long grey fish drifts above
the soft floor over the leaves
returning to their previous lives

it looks into the centre of spores
clustered under the tree fern fronds with eyes
trying to forget

High above where I have never lived

a thornbill jets through the twigs
and the rufus whistlers begin their territorial
alarms—So I am finally here
watching my face searching for the next mask

In the house my wife is moving behind
sheets of glass holding the pages of sleep
I can't read—she awaits

the time we have been trying for
the moments without wings we can never own
she looks out at my face

It is a life I am unable to recall or imagine

In the house among the spotted gums
my face has been up all night talking to itself
speaking in tongues

crashing about in the living room
a bowerbird caged-in growing weak
in panic howling

Here in the bush it makes no sound
the eyes join the moving sky
and the mouth draws in more air for its lies

the black tongue a broken wing
and the beaked nose a dorsal before the chin's bristle

I try to remember a face in a language
we speak trees in

An Elm Tree in Paddington

Branches of grapevine thick as ankles
grow through the terrace-iron,
the fruit is a bitter wood; I think

of Brennan standing on similar joinery,
in the same suburb, soured by love
and Symbolism. A black beetle waves

a feeler, its lasso, involves itself
with the security mesh before the panes
of rain-printed glass. I drink

American whisky from a champagne flute
and think of Lawson at the Rose & Crown,
he knew the price of a beer

cost more than the blackest sonnet.
The drinkers choose not to hear
parody in a voice, see the rag of a suit,

know the terrible hour it took
to shave up and comb for this sad front.
Out in the yard an old elm shoots

out from the acid dirt at an angle,
its boughs spokes of sylvan thought, here
where form eats content to a gloss.

Gutting the Salmon

The blade touches the fish heart, over
the kitchen floor, over the newspaper
its body meat; the cat circles
the outside edges of blood-drenched type,
the boys look on, taking it in—
This isn't like weekend fishing, cleaning
other fish: down into the nets of veins,
severed arteries; the ritual goes on
out of control—fillets of red meat, fillets
of white, flesh almost black
dark blue with blood; the cat now howling
its Burmese meat-mantra, the boys
turning to TV football. No feeling
of remorse though how to stop, how to clean up;
back into the content of the gut, husks
of prawn, fragments of worm; the liver spilling
through fingers.

Tasmania

One night in swamp-land
on an outcrop thick
with bottlebrush
inside a sandstone cradle
I came across a devil
its rank cave
a nest of skeletons
its thick pelt
a pattern of red fleck
its legs striped
a voice cackled out
from its whiskered head
and its eyes were
tiny miner's lanterns
I slowly backed away in starlight
now a marsupial growls
under my thumb as I type
its fierce presence
voice-prints
its reminding eyes
phrased in a map of language
traced on a page.

Memory Walks

Ideas of memory walks
replace our need for narrative
Our heads flicker projecting their stories

There's a boat at the end of each tale
and the weary can just paddle out
onto the stream

water sparkling with minerals good enough to drink
Each stroke of the oar stains it
with the inky clouds of thinking

Here we come across the node
of the fractured sentence that indicates
an overload so we dump our ballast of loves

There's a couple of lives
and the brave among us can choose both
The consequences are there each morning

flaring away in the bathroom mirror
staring over the coffee and toast
the space where lovers come clean

about their strolls
and what they scratched on public walls
the night before

Domestic Shuffle

A bike with one wheel buckled, the other
slowly turning in the wind, feathers
scattered around its circumference, caged
finches squeaking near the sandpit where the

children play. When a woman in the laundry
doorway starts flapping her wings, the little
girl chases the cat, the boy starts yelling—
it's morning, it's still in the morning.

Button your lips and swallow, keep
those words from rumbling out. They're from the
Bible: turn the page in your head
and say to yourself forgive, for God's sake

forgive and forget, there's nothing to be said.
A hand lashes out, words making a noise,
and suddenly your mother's hand's slapping your face
hard. You can't remember the actual sting, the shock

and pain the hand inflicted. Now forgive
its meaning: put your hand into water as hot
as you can bear it—the throbbing will fade as the water
cools, like poison from a red rock cod.

Nothing repeats itself, not even heat. Time
is not time, music not music, even Wagner's
Tristan und Isolde playing from the quarterdeck,
even this domestic shuffle that continues as we speak.

Winter Night

ᴐ *for Kevin Hart*

In the darkness beyond our garden fence,
a white-tailed water rat. Our cat crouches
in ambush in the mango tree. Down
below, an amateur fisherman flicks a lure

at racks of oysters near the shore,
then gives up and takes a swig of whisky.
Ah, the way that first drink braces.
A motorboat roars by—no lights—

the black river swallows it, leaving
behind a swirl of fumes. The surface
reflects the glow from our house
and the chuckling call of a nightjar.

Stars fracture the sky with light. The cat
keeps playing with weird marsupials,
the hook wound in my finger stings
like hell. As I come up from the wharf,

a flying fox rattles in the banana palms—
I hear the long whisper of its beating wings
follow me up the stairs. The stars flicker
letters from a dead god's alphabet.

The Ravens: After Trakl

The ravens launch themselves
into the air

dropping harsh calls as they
sail across midday:

their shadows follow them
along the glassy river—

you can see them at times
almost resting.

They rupture the silence
at twilight. At other times

their sound is like the stench
of drunks bickering over

carrion in the beer garden.
Look up into the spotted

gum tree: they fly off
like a funeral procession,

their caws small shudders
of rapture.

What I Have of Faith

If you look out
the window you will see nothing
the willow is flowing nicely

you will be blind
and hear the sound of poetry
read by a woman

who reviews owls, like an owl
split in two by a cat, flying off
in two directions

on this side, a sprig of inkweed
on the other, Tasmanian kelp.
Here language comes out

at night and mixes
with the locals, who knows what
is getting done

aside from talking.
The serious tone is more assuring
well, more than laughter—

for some reason things
change tonight, we hear a muted
thudding, a good night

for the litter of kittens.
Hawks circle the kitchen light,
moths with beaks

come flying out, nothing
surreal. The lawn man walks in
with a glad-bag

dropping feathers; you must
remember to reassemble the goldfinch
before the refreshments.

Percy Grainger Waltz

I come bringing news
from the bitter
nights at Balmoral,
right on the beach
where I left
the torn pages—
flowering platitudes,
exhausted similes,
the way we seem
to cling to
a semblance
of description.
I went my way
slashing the phrases,
tearing apart
picture-books
looking for something
of substance.
Look at this bleak
riff-raff calling
themselves the poetry
of bliss: you'll
hear a nasty melody
as I cut your
tongues out, there
the saturnine comfort
in the deed undone—

torn apart and put
back together
as an absolutely different
animal, a slug
pushing its fat way
across the purple
skin of an overipe
eggplant. I was
further up the beach
by the time I thought
I could actually
hear myself talking
to the woman,
looking into her
eyes I saw blue and
empty canyons.

The Australian Crawl

I watched your body fluttering across
the pool, your hands little buckets
chucking water on the flames. The bushfire
was background music as the kids

sploshed about in the wading area—
all this time and we believed our bodies
meant something, life at least.
Birthdays shivered up our spines,

sparks in the pallid undergrowth of hair
greying and uncurling. In this dream
our first picnic sails along
on a blanket just above the flames,

the women wearing gingham frocks
making it seem so very sad, Uncle John
juggling his belly on a tricycle,
the bacon-rind on the sliced bread

a wizened hieroglyph meaning nothing,
the cucumber circles sitting on the sockets
of your mother's eyes. Back at home
on the shelf conch-shells

sitting next to books become
little inkwells of nasty belief,
the silver we never used dancing
on the table like soft silver tadpoles—

sequential meanings drift into meltdown.
The pale-headed rosella's a smudge
on the bathroom mirror, the whole house
is full of an awful music chuffing

and percussing in your head—
a rat-a-tat and an Australian threadfin
salmon comes down south while you're
fishing hookless in the sky.

A picture becomes three-dimensional: it's
Tassie the cat, fleas scooting down his tail
into the fish tank. Outside cockatoos
flurry, inside a Wettex shivers in the sink.

THE STONE CURLEW

ᴣ

Ways of looking at twenty-one birds

The Stone Curlew

I am writing this inside the head
of a bush stone curlew,
we have been travelling for days

moving over the earth
flying when necessary.
I am not the bird itself, only its passenger

looking through its eyes.
The world rocks slightly as we move
over the stubble grass of the dunes,

at night shooting stars draw lines
across the velvet dark
as I hang in a sling of light

between the bird's nocturnal eyes.
The heavens make sense, seeing this way
makes me want to believe

words have meanings,
that Australia is no longer a wound
in the side of the earth.

I think of the white settlers
who compared the curlew's song
to the cries of women being strangled,

and remember the poets who wrote
anthropomorphically as I sing softly
from the jelly of the stone curlew's brain.

The Yellow Bittern

At Uladulla
a bittern puffs out its neck feathers,
head between wings—

slits of eyes tight in the wind
flinging sand, hammering grains of stone
against it.

Our bird of words falls apart—
its wings without vowels,
its head empty of tough money.

O bittern, come off it, talk to us
about when we were young: that first
kiss hissing as she bit my tongue.

The Jesus Bird

The lotus-bird's signature
is slenderness, moving

without ring-marking water's
skin-tight surface.

A colourist, strokes tone
with a wing, fans out pinions:

The show's to escape
death in shape of harrier

or swamp's light-slashing pike.
The night watch is a dance

where bird antenna
probes mind-stepping illusions

to parry with a stray
plug-throwing fisherman,

alert in thin air
whirred by a dragonfly's

cellophane propeller,
or puttering swamp-bugs.

When the creek's back is dark
glass, a conjurer, striper,

lotus-dancing with river-pimps.
Creek alley's side-show.

Crows in Afternoon Light

How close can a human get to a crow,
how much do we know about them?
It's good to know we'll never read their brains,
never know what it means to be a crow.

All those crow poems are about poets—
none of them get inside the crow's head,
preen or rustle, let alone fly on crow wings.

No one knows what it is to sing crow song.

Five crows hop and stand around
the fish I have left for them on the wharf.
If I move their eyes follow me. I stand still
and they pick up a fish, test its weight,

then ruffle their feathery manes and shine.

These black bird shapes outlined by light,
behind them the river flowing out, the light
changing—soon it will be night

and they will be gone. Before that
I praise crows.

The Great Knot

Alterant birds, alterant words
and Bunting's descant on a madrigal,
Zukofsky's 'descrying black-hellebore

white white double flowered
marsh-mallow mallow-rose
snowstorm sea-hollyhock'

and you're dancing with words in particular.
This bird's a traveller, summers
in north-eastern Siberia,

winters in southern China
and has vagrants that fly to Australia.
Zukofsky's flowers are words in bloom

strung out along the song lines,
the great knot as tricky as whisky
running along whisky-coloured shores

where clear water laps granite
and salt water foams on the sandstone.
Its shadow shoots over lagoons

rancid with verbiage in disintegration
as it tries to describe the sink ponds of paper mills,
factories discharging, alterant poems.

The Southern Skua

The skua flew into our heads in 1968—
a new kind of poetry, a scavenging predator
frequently attacking humans,
flying through the streets of seaside towns,
foraging with seagulls. This bird
has few predators. One was found
in Tasmania, its beak embedded in the skull
of a spotted quoll, dragged
into a clearing by devils. They form clubs
and proclaim their territory
by various displays and loud aggressive calls;
they are agile metaphysicians,
sweeping along lines of projective verse,
echoing each other's songs.
Although the skua breeds on Black Mountain
it is migratory and dispersive, its call
a series of low quacks and thin whinnying squeals.
They are omnivorous and critical creatures;
animal liberationists never mention
the habits of skua. If you read skua poetry, beware:
one could fly out from the page
and change the expression on your face.

The Pheasant-tailed Jacana

The canoe wings its way upstream.
A school of garfish scatter
around lily-pads, streaking

silver pencils, scribbling nonsense;
their gut-sacks translucent,
alive with insect larvae, calligraphic ink.

Green and difficult, wet
feathers trailing, the jacana draws
lines of cobweb through sunlight

picking off spinning dragonflies;
air bubbles rise from the mouth
of a lungfish under its surface stepping feet.

Maybe an image of the jacana
comes to the insane remembering Jesus.
Up here in the jungle

we see flowers glowing,
smelling as sweet in the fist of a drunk,
stumped for meaning, grumbling

back at his own face reflected
on a flowing sheet of the creek's surface.
Leaping back into the picture, stepping out

with its long tail held high
for no reason but instinct, its eyes drawing in
shapes we cannot know.

Arctic Jaeger

This bird comes between the light
and your reading, hang-glides
in a corner of your eye, a pirate

with a feather in its cap—a sly con
riding the breath of your best line;
flying straight out of Olson's delirium tremens

hangs around with dead fish
under its wing; heavier than a night heron
like a loose-winged falcon:

take its shape to mean blood sport
on our terms. Lines drawn from the breath,
one flash of meaning following

another, a bad draft in its claw
a quote from Cohen's *The Future*
in its bill—this bird cuts out descriptions,

its flight over bleak oceans
tells no story, its white plumage a flying page
written in a language not endangered.

The Upland Sandpiper

*ॐ The Upland Sandpiper scrapes into the list of Australian
birds on the strength of but one record. The bird, 'Shot by
an old sportsman, during the snipe seasons of 1848, near the
water reservoir in the vicinity of Sydney,' was sent to John
Gould in London by the Committee of Superintendence of the
Australian Museum in Sydney.* —JOHN DOUGLAS PRINGLE

When it comes to earth it lands on airfields.
Maybe it remembers its original haunts,
the American prairies—the bird
books say it is 'gregarious at all seasons,
though often encountered alone.'
The upland sandpiper breeds in Alaska
and winters in South America; this bird
is the totem animal of the Australian poet
Anthony Lawrence. It makes only long-distance
calls to James Dickey, knowing it would
be shot by him on sight. Although
this bird is a distant relative of the
stone curlew it does not have a square head
and its eyes are the colour of live bait;
it shoots out of existence if forced onto
paper; some say it can read the handwriting
of the reeds in a pond in Clarksburg, Ontario.
Another theory is that John Gould
invented it—so that this bird exists only
on paper. Recently I heard a lyrebird
mimicking its call, a series of mellow
whistling trills, echoing over the incoming
tide on the Hawkesbury River.

The Hudsonian Godwit

Although it breeds in Hudson Bay,
it winters in South America.
However, a lone vagrant godwit
was found at Kooragang Island
in New South Wales before
the Christmas of 1982—word
spread quickly and many observers
travelled to Newcastle to see it.
They are still searching. This
Australian godwit's call—toy, toy, toy—
was recorded and this recording
has been compared to the work
of Phil Spector. Its markings are
complex and beautiful, with
prominent white supercilium,
dorsum deep grey with each feather
fringed white, its underparts mainly
soot-grey. It is a bird for objectivists.
It wades through the shallows,
its bill making rapid stitching motions
as it sews together its own wake.
The godwit's cryptic markings
make it a perfect object for the similes
of Australia's 'greatest imagist'—
but don't look, you won't find it.

The Cow Bird

This is not poetry—this bird's turkey-head
has a craw that produces crap—its chicks,
      feeding, get covered in a stench
      you could compare

to the breath of an alcoholic cane toad
that's feasted on a bucket of rancid pork.
      The descriptive drift
      throws up this internationalist:

the hoatzin (pronounced what-seen)
lives on the banks of the Orinoco River
      flowing through the central
      plains of Venezuela.

Young hoatzins dive-bomb the surface
from their nests overhead, swim
      underwater then pull themselves
      back up into the trees

with their clawed wing-tips.
The idea of these creatures has been known
      to drive scientific investigators
      crazy: infesting the imaginations

of phytochemists from within,
they create themselves from the dark
      whims of their hosts, parachuting
      in through their eyes.

Good students have fried their brains
contemplating the mating habits
        of the cowbird—they are, however, pure
        joy to confessional poets,

who weave them in as tropes as they write poems
concerning their wedding night, in which they
        consummate their bliss oozing
        the milk of what-seens.

Red-necked Avocet

Wading in a lake, its entrance
to the sea blocked, our legs
illuminated by white-hot
mantles burning kerosene
in pressure lamps, it was all
detail. Could we know
the avocets were victims?
The acid from our joint
imagination billowed
behind us, a killing wake:
we were all eyes. Huge prawns
kicked up under our toes,
then zapped away into weeds;
the wings of black swans fanned
our desire to eat the avocet's
fragile, mottled eggs. We tried
to feed one of the chicks
boiled prawns; she looked
angelic as she shuddered.
The fire on the sand crackled
with dead bulrush canes and spat
whizzing, popcorn-sized embers;
flames licked the black
of the moon. Our cotton clothes
soaked up the smoke's breath.
We were drunk with salt
and sand, with killing, eating
prawns, talking rubbish, having
fun. Avocets migrated from our
thoughts into sound as they
too became human.

Major Mitchell's Pink Cockatoo

In the Mallee, dodging crooked branches of mulga
trees, she waits like a sundial for our caravan,
her clear voice a distinct falsetto attracting
passion police and painted quail. Time the cracker
keeps her harmful—her sweat's a fixative, printing alluring
shadows on skin, sketches intricate with pain. We track her
by the dark tan wickerwork winds make of her nests.
The world crumbles into red sand as she takes
my place—neither bird nor feathered tease
of her flock—and I walk out, prepared to let fall—
look—my frame, tail-shaped, fanning air.
Getting nowhere.

Eclectus Parrot

Bright green, scarlet-bellied, black-billed bird
crash lands in campsite. Fire burns cub's fingers.
The scoutmaster flicks the billy with a switch
and growls. Smoke billows and turns brown.

This picture-on-a-biscuit-tin is being
painted as we read: the politician as artist
on his weekend fishing trip. His son,
an eagle scout, hammers the billy

with a triangle. Now hundreds
of budgerigars wheel across a low sky:
the whole jumble's put together from used
landscapes garnished with raptors.

The Minister of Defence has news for these
creatures. He mimics the eclectus parrot—
his face turns red like its satin belly—but his
black beak's genetically engineered for speech.

Gang-Gang Cockatoos

In the outer suburbs we pass under them,
dark grey with white stripes, in swishing
fractals of tropical vegetation,
screeching metal songs,

swinging upside down, juggling
pine-nuts—very funny but beyond us.
My state of mind's stencilled on the
footpath, my footprints identical

to gang-gangs': there's a crevice in my
forehead, with a slash of grey, but overall my
head's a red hood. As for my tremulous
tone of voice, who'd believe such

flickering convictions? I smile because
things are so pleasant here: my lightweight
cotton top's cool on humid days, and the
southerly each afternoon

ruffles my feathers, so that sometimes
I chuckle. Since my children left New
York and set up house in exclusive
suburbs—well? The colossal

phone bills, the visits maybe once
in three years, snaps of the kids dressed
as gang-gang chicks in a delightful garden,
the daughter-in-law pecking for money,

private schools to teach them 'Hello Cocky'
—it's 'swell.' I've never used that word,
just wanted to indicate I'm familiar
with the tone used in the cages

of middle America. Gang-gang women
know the score and take it on the chin:
we scorn the first person singular because
at night we drift beyond it.

The Ruff

It's difficult to describe the ruff.
This bird's a live metaphor, puffing
its plumage into simile. A rough
attempt at meaning: though a
waterbird, it dances onshore.

Its colours? Sepia, cream, and
specks of red. These tones bleed well
for watercolourists, but a cock ruff
in display looks top-heavy, often
toppling over into absurdity or worse.

Ruff's a word from the sixteenth century:
feathers goffered into ornaments
for sex. Ritual is human. These cock
birds blow up by instinct, strutting
as if to get across how inhuman

they are, how utterly bird. They
dance in lines of ruff music; some
have suggested that a feather's cadence,
once heard, conducts this dance—
a puffed pose, its head hidden by dark

cowling and the eyes blinded by display.
The ruff's ways delight us if we have
a sense of humour or a dash of
madness: the way of the ruff
is for folk who take themselves

seriously, for this bird's habits
contradict words, art, and human
silence. A ruff occurs at the fringes
of things, in the gap between it
and words. Ruff.

The Grey Whistler

There's a man knocking at the door.
He was a friend once; these days
he's on his last legs—body and soul

stitched together by the court of petty
sessions, he makes a living serving writs.
Samples of deliverance are considered

by the jurists, so I provide details
of my shame—by drawing, for example,
a tropical whistler. Once called the brown

whistler, it lives in mangrove swamps
and their adjoining rainforests. This bird
creates hatches in dense foliage: you can

reach into them and salvage a shabby
pillow of whistler-down created by
tropical humidity, as soft as the texture

of human sorrow. Our friend's ex-wife
was a model who pranced the catwalks
in gowns embroidered with luminous

flecks from the whistler's pinions—
the handiwork of that one-eyed Italian
who made his name in Paris. I have some

fabric in a basket—let's turn it into a hood.
Next time he knocks, I'll pull it over my
head and act dumb. Peggy, there's a good

girl, stay calm—I'm a husk each time
you wince. But the knocking at the door
continues. In the backyard lemon tree,

there's a city crow coughing its lungs up.
As the night goes on, the man outside
becomes the Grey Whistler.

The Dollarbird

As the family listened to the reading
of the will, dollarbirds were landing,
summer migrants thudding into soft
magnolia trees in bloom. It seems
I'll be able to free this captive life
of my mind, let it fall from my eyes
like fish scales and just walk away—
now she'll be okay financially at least.

My conscience, the bully, keeps honing
these blunt threats daily. How much
freedom will she take, how many lozenges
of grief in brown paper bags? I'll scatter
rotten fruit on the terrace and every flying
insect on the northern peninsula will loop
and scuttle in droves for the feast. Dollarbirds

will hawk for them in the air. Translucent,
she glides through my thoughts reading
The Divine Comedy in the compartment
I've filed her in. Bad? Sure, but there's more
housework to be done in my head today.
Pawpaws rot efficiently—they attract pests
from miles away, hovering and crawling.

As she listens, her cheeks glow, her thoughts
swerve as elegantly as dollarbirds, gathering
the words to strike. There's a cavil, a hiccup
and a shudder down her spine. Thirty years
of gibberish, resentments drenched in perfume,
years of love and an inkling she could be wrong.

Can I siphon off the fertilising fantasy and let
passion wither like old skin? Unpleasant
metaphors vanish, migrate back to where
those green-feathered beakies come from:
a dollarbird tumbles as it flies above
magnolia trees in bloom.

The Red-bearded Bee-eater

The swinging gate to the resort
was a rickety affair, its hinges
sang to the ratchet-throated bowerbirds.
The atmosphere was thousand years
thick as I pushed through
the crumbling day: then green
wings opened and I was away—
The surf thumped against a beach,
children scrambled in a nearby park
pulling strings controlling
a huge rice-paper bird flapping
along the grass. A man in a monk's
habit walked out of the bush
handed me a pair of gloves
with orders to pull weeds.
Sure I'm having a drink now, it's
already dark but no oblivion—
there's a burning hell in my head,
and I can't make out the birds
from fruit bats in this paradise
of palm trees. Finally my wife
and children carried me
to our quarters—I woke at dawn,
feeling alive I walked about,
I opened the bathroom cupboard,
there was a bare wall at its back
and in the plaster a red-bearded bee-eater
had drilled a hollow for its nest:
inside two chicks rolled their big heads
and squawked for bees.

Rainbow Bee-eaters

Their wings fuelled
by a knowledge of bees,

turning on axles of air,
each crescent beak

an orange-coloured talisman
Once snowy-headed elders

gathered honey bags
in turpentine forests

feathery blurs eating bees
hovering miracles

alongside ancient cliffs
flashed brightly

Your film exposed to them
transparencies

to stay love by catching day
light on pages

the translucent calligraphy
of wings

Kingfishers Appearing

A circle of blue falls over
a kingfisher, an exercise in ink

control—its flight out of mist
plunges me into the day.

I pull the tide in empty, feel again
the hollow pit in my chest, craving

the uncertainty of night.
Waking beside you, always

dropped from nowhere into this bed—
How does it happen? The sheets

full of light, my head riddled with dark.
Grace is radiance as

I reach over, my arms full
of branches where the kingfisher

doesn't alight, where
no mist drifts. In a climate of silence

an indigo space filled
by the flight of the bird,

my days fluttering pages
falling through the kingfisher's life.

A FUTURE BOOK

ॐ

Letters to poets, myths and writing writing

Walking by the River

He walked waist-deep
through his thoughts,
emotions, a tangle of vines
and tree-creepers.

His words were finches,
flying before him
as he swung his arms—
scrambled paragraphs.

A waterfall sounded
ahead of his walk,
chipped words cracked
with each step. He came to

a calm place, opulent phrases
in bloom: purple-fruited
pigface, the blackthorn's
blue-black sloe.

American Sonnet

᷆ for John Forbes

I am the snow bandit who must travel
in the red dirt night, this hat is
for style more than anything, shade
amuses me, or the idea of shade
I should say as no such thing exists
in the spirit world of talk. I wrestle
butterflies of light with my gaze,
these strange tracks that I leave
are for the anthropologist of morning;
ash fills my pockets as I fold away
sheets of anything resembling thought;
all I go by is the way it feels, no
thing bothers me unless it hurts.
I don't know what worship is for, let
alone what it is—I tried once in
swampland to the north of here to
describe talk, no such luck, no
such pain, yes even words perish
from lack of care, lack of use.

Waving to Hart Crane

Farewell to the wire,
the voices on
the line. Goodbye
switchboard rider, my

American friend.
We enter the new
century through glass,
black oceans

and black winds,
thin fibre funnelling
poetry out
of existence.

No sonnet will survive
the fax on fire,
out-sound that hash
of voices slung up

from the cable.
Tip your hat
and flicker with
smoke from silent movies,

there are no more
cunning gaps left
on the cutting room
floor by editors.

Here they expunge
the message, nothing's
praise. If gestures
appear they fold in fade-out.

A Future Book

Among birds shaped by the stars
I reached through branches,
a levitating feather
difficult to grasp.

The editor pumped for facts,
there's no story here,
just the drifting pinion
and my fingers working

its shaft: I use the lake
as an inkwell, draw
invisible serifs.
Catbirds loop through

the casuarina spray,
I cannot tell you where I am—
somewhere in the bloodstream
is all I can say. My voice

is parched as ink hits the air,
day itself is the only page.
In the lake a bird wades,
its call a swishing of bone.

Daybook for Eurydice

A sprig of delphinium

She saw hoops in his eyes, behind the brown
cordage of opaque veins, wheels of light.
I believed him. In this fashionable precinct
there is a café where the pagans hang out—

the perpendicular city shoots up and the sky
is smudged across the window, a bevy of road-peckers
rule the roost but don't worry, if anyone
walks in on us maybe they'll skid into

an imbroglio and have some gratuitous fun.
If gender is a foreign language, let's drop
expectations, sleight of word and be impetuous.

Take this sprig of delphinium, my chatterbox,
our lives will change.

Raining italics

He travels heavy, lopsided, slanting home,
leaving behind the scene in the café.
What's pertinent now? What type of flower
will shoot from his eye when he endeavours

to create his paradise? He walks the streets
of the inner city enduring his limbo, calm as a sentence
not including weather. When he trundles
through the gates he knows there will

be phosphor-headed floozies and acceptance.
He remembers his mother pruning geraniums;
he played in her garden with his hoop

and watched the rainbow. Time is fascinating
yet vile. The rain creates acrid fumes.

The transcribed hoop

We are lines in a hand-coloured lithograph.
We watch a hoop trying to bowdlerise itself.
Strange markings. These lines have been
forced onto the paper, you can read the result

of the printer's pathetic yodelling—in the small hours
he practised his calligraphy, his imagination's
gyrating tonnage. His scribbling was a fine
exercise until he decided to transcribe it.

What his ebullient inspiration amounted to was
simply heavy doodling. Every day he said: tomorrow.
He'd frame it up and make a presentation—

a Valentine, he'd tear his chest apart. Self-critical to a t,
he rolled it up, posting off a tube.

The visible, the untrue

This room has existed for all these years in
Edmund Spenser's head, a gnome works
there on an etching of a hummock. His
first sketch was drawn from life one day

as he lay out by the juniper attending to those
details that nature did omit, breaking bread mixed in
with Edmund's 'substance base.' True Jonathan
does some kind of a dance and raves.

The Faerie Queene is a drag show bedecked and scored
with synthetic cloth and acrylic glitter, they eat
the drumsticks of the bird of paradise:

their great ideals have been mollified by grim lust,
their geodesic discotheque is held together by art alone.

The bower of bliss

Birds, voices, instruments, winds, waters
all agree: the windpipe created a melodious tone
as the blade sunk home. Although sorcery
is not in fashion it worked. The mask of Cupid fell,

revealing a man without a hat, a murderous
swine cold as a jobfish. If we translate the circuitous
murmuring of hoops bowled along, if we
squint, a picture will form from the sounding:

it will turn out to be the blonde woman
from *Blonde on Blonde*, the sad-eyed lady herself—
she has a rendezvous tomorrow, under a juniper tree

with a landscape painter. They'll exchange sketches.
Outside on the street drunks are shadow-boxing neon.

Nothing on the mind

The gnome's Akubra is part of his head.
He drinks Jack & Coke—at last they've come up
with an alcoholic robot. Let me tell you
ambition leads to imitation oak.

The weight of eyes rides on my cheeks,
until blotchy flowers become thoughts
feeding by brain; venomous butterflies flit
through my eardrums. When the limits fall away,

brightness flares about, there is no shade—
nothing but illumination on a sea of drink.
Philosophers I swallowed undigested swim in circles,

bronze-whalers of the intellect, you can't dream
in this slipstream of blood. Your punishment is to think.

Our different versions

Everybody thinks they've been in hell too long,
it's the quality of the shades you meet.
I'm fond of the ones who say we're underground,
maybe it's the language of the inferno

that keeps it bearable. Or the letters home.
Then his voice over-riding the morning:
I'll give you one last song that will explain everything.
Some girl's been walking naked in the bedroom,

softly howling for an hour. She's not out of it,
just a bit tight, who wants to spoil the night?
Hell has no location. There's a swirl of information

and we notice the details on the edges. Stay hear me sing.
An old song is scratching the tissue of the drum.

The sepia hummock

She threw open the window and light dappled
the furniture, it made the artifact
leachy and banal. It came in a tube.
The fellow from Edmund Spenser's head

had sent her his etching of a hummock, it wasn't
pushing the envelope of landscape, it was
simply a weird twist in the narrative. Can you
stalk yourself? Her morning fell apart,

she forgot to feed the baby barramundi in
their tank for the restaurant, the dish-washer
imploded. Simple tasks became operatic. A man

on a talkback radio show was grunting. She turned
the volume up. The amplifier blew a tweeter.

She speaks, language falls apart

I cannot remain silent and outside time
any longer, this city just repeats itself
wars and people come and go. Pigeons and rats
stay the same, the blue-bar fans his tail

and does his two-step with sound effects,
in the rain his breast throws out its rainbow, he bobs
and runs and gets reassuring rejections. I want
to focus on some particular time and place,

drink *Split Rock* mineral water and talk.
Wasted, wasted on time, wasted eloquence,
rhetoric can get you out of hell, barbaric song

can brace your soul, can be equivocal as pigeon talk.
All I am is words, human song, a noise that edges in.

At the ferry, the tide

Who is Eurydice under the stars? One night I stood
naked on a pylon of the wharf—as the ferries
came close, we'd dive just in front of them,
and as we swam, the water flowed through us.

Particles, we streamed through the
symbiotic tide—our cells, phosphorescent,
came up churned and laughing from that
dangerous wake. No Eurydice but playing out

the myth: there's a boatman waiting where
the memory fades. Our lovers, drunk, sang for tourists,
fluking coins with the drugs and wine.

It was bracing to live in that paradise
as lucidity cut through the wax.

Song

We all know the past can't interleave
with now, I fly into this. Now outside
the harbour flows into morning—
walking on sand, swimming in air,

the texture of flowers exploding with satin
bowerbirds, rainbow lorikeets and the
seduction of perfumes, the tides
full of mullet bouncing from glassy

water, leatherjackets sucking at pylons,
butterflies in the magnolias, kids flying a kite
and that airliner shimmering under the red sky.

My love, today I'll catch you a silver dory
and tonight, grill it with lemon and a pinch of salt

Coda: the nightjar

Seems weird a bird Aristotle talked about
lives here, the nightjar
Aegotheles cristatus, crested goatsucker,

under the city in a deserted railway station,
a great white cave. The electricity
has been cut and it is completely dark.

She flies out along the air ducts
up into the city's towers,
eating moths along the way.

The nightjar, according to Aristotle,
would fly out over the country
and find goats to drink from their teats.

Eurydice flies up from under the ground
and moves through the penthouses,
her white wings stroking polished atmosphere

going from bed to bed, changing form,
listening for her lover's song.

Letter to Robert Creeley

I've heard the system's closing down. It's good
reading in books, old friend, your words about

what a friend is, if you have one. These
days I often think of Zukofsky
just throwing in the word

'objectivist' and how it works
as well as any label could. These

days we're just words away
from death and I think

I've finally learnt to listen (your love
songs seem wise now that the years

have steadied my head) as you turn hurt
without sentiment to gain. I thought

of your clear humour when my father
was dying of cancer. I asked about the pain

and he spun me a line: 'It feels like a big
mud crab having a go at my spine.'

The Flow-through

> for the Johns

We loved the front, your wall of words,
and the fact that snatches made
sense to the professors. We read
The Double Dream of Spring

and argued fiercely about whether
this was the way to go—tied knots
in your tangles, tendrils of phrases

that wound their way round our pages.
Those were the days we exist in now—
we hacked through time

and came out twisted. Gaping holes
in space, we fed on sentences stitched
together with a grammar that was streetwise,

though with impeccable manners that always
got us through the gates. The mix of sweetness
and a ferocity that could burn holes

was what I admired most in *Some Trees*—
Those poems were places I made friends in.
I remember Tranter standing in a classroom

reading them, his laughter edged with
irony and kindness. Ashbery days, when poets
were drunk on code within code,

when language cracked open and showed us
the power of whimsy and a dark abyss
that said 'perhaps' as it echoed.

Letter to Tom Raworth

Before escaping
from the clock
self imposes
on the page
in those days
I could hardly talk
and called you
in my head Tom
Raw Worth
There was some
kind of criminal
in a poem of yours
called Morrell
Moving's rich
brown endpapers
were doors
I slunk through
and lived there
free from narrative
speaking language
I could read not utter
The light led me
through chambers
of murmurings
calling me
I thought in the
pitch of your voice
though it was
streets not spires

where books
were not blocks
of stone or holy glass
but a sly side of the
mouth code
serious song
that wouldn't
parry or fuck
with you
for exclaiming
these lines are
wonderful these
tough folk are not
embarrassed by wonder
Morrell's keys to
the prison jingled
as you walked up walls
your head took
the weight and made
the weirdness
surrounding me
release small change
to pay for sheets
of creamy Fabriano
that were soon
transformed into
a kind of folding
money so the
Morrells could
pay for their keys
and on each page
I made appeared
that watermark *Raw Worth*

The Bunker

My walls are made of fish scales, we slip
through words, fissures, cracks
in the radiance. Outside the slot of air
that is our window, phrases
from French and English fleck the night

with whatever we are.
We expect poems to catch
what words can't; talk of life breaks in,
filleting the code, a syllable's blade,
a fish, a cold hand—so we create

sonnets of skin, little bunkers for emergencies,
spikes of meaning inside them
parting the river of words.
In times of peace we drift down rivers
through countries and into oceans.

We fish for sirens, then discuss fishing
with them—it's a fine thing to do
in the real sea with living fish to kill and eat,
our words lures spinning
in their heads. Though once you start

thinking about it you're sunk,
there's no simulacrum, you can't construct
meanings for fishing—you can
fashion a fish trap though,
weld wire into a cage or hoop—but there's no

welding the wires in your head.
Take some flesh and thread it onto
a chemically sharpened hook, the offshore
Gamakatsu—is there any vernacular
clarity in that? At night under the stars

we just do it, poems flow—
next morning the talk seems stupid
as you stand, water dribbling through the holes
in your big dipper, about to be rust
more scales forming—in the gammer of sun.

Black Water

I took Robert Duncan in my grandfather's skiff
rowing across Mooney Creek
words hummed around our heads

The trees are speaking on the far shore
we'll never get there in time
the pages of books swim upstream

we study words growing on them
The time will come and you will turn
the present a breeze that passes

carrying the smell of cut grass
The Mower is creating as he moves through
the rushes looking for glow-worms

Words little warm animals of air
words growing and teaming over the mudflats
This river has no bends

this river is not an actual river yet
this water has eaten its way into sandstone
great sheets of it slide by on either side

parting and taking the flotsam
'for she my mind hath so displaced
that I shall never find my home'

Marvell was calling from the mangroves
time created endless bends

the river was never the same
that night Duncan gathered the southern stars
into his being the black water plopping with fat mullet

Letter to Eurydice

Watercolour moon, the window-panes
fogged up. Outside, the river

slips by; an overhanging blackbutt
branch inscribes the surface

with a line across foaming run-off.
Living near mudflats I'm protected

by mangroves: in winter
the southerly rakes their curly heads,

the green skirts are my windbreak.
At the Fork these summer thoughts

are silted up and become obscure:
it's more than halfway into a big ebb

and my mind's a dark moat. If you
get this far—watch it—and step

on my dreams, you'll find
they've been pulped. It's only flight

that matters here; take a break and fling
your next thought into the tide.

In these parts, the lyrebird must carry
its own cage on its back

through swamps—I once believed this.
But yesterday the bird suffered a stroke.

'It keeps falling to the ground,' the ranger
said, 'nothing can be done.' It's time

to commiserate with this creature,
all songbird but not quite lyre.

Eurydice and the Mudlark

Sunlight fades the coloured spine
of *What Bird Is That?* The shadow

of your hand marks my face:
wings and the tips of fingers,

coiled hands in the tiny egg
or sac of living tissue,

dredge up a likeness beyond
appearance. Morning unfurls,

I wake and shave. In the mirror
the reflection of a mudlark's tail-fan

echoes the silence of glass.
We hover all day on the surface

of the stream, above a soft bottom,
until moonlight falls again

onto stark white bed-sheets.
The shadow your hand casts

resembles the mudlark, opening
its wings, calling and rocking,

perched in the pages
of my book.

The Floating Head

I turned off electricity, pulled telephone cords
out of the wall, saw stars in glass through cedar slats.
I wrapped a scarf around my headache
and looked inside—

an ebbing memory leaving with the tide.
My boat's motor roared and I hurtled across
the river into blazing cold night
then circled back.

Crouched in a corner of the house,
my cat borrows my voice—I talk
to him through the night. The heater
clicks, its pilot light blinks. I scribble

a few lines, pass my fishing rod off
as a lyre. Who needs this bitter tune?
Its distorted chords lull me into numbness.
I bend it over double and pluck.

Eurydice Agape

A preacher came to Calabash Creek
in an expensive four-wheel drive.
He set up in the little park
with his team of technicians.
Bose speakers hung from the gum trees.
The kookaburras started laughing
just before dark.

An oyster farmer's punt, full of
drunks from the Workers Club,
took off from the mudflats and roared
into the night. They called us a bunch
of cunts. Before long the children
from the point were speaking
in tongues. The singing

was fabulous—a woman sang
the Statesboro Blues—and there
was talk of miracles. Then the
preacher spoke of Hell. Suddenly
my arms were full, you started
sobbing, my face was wet with tears.
You were back in paradise.

The Serpent

Twenty crows gathered on a branch,
bare in the early summer's heat.
We strung a bow from the willow tree

and used bamboo for arrows.
The afternoon thrummed with locusts.
Clouds at the end of the sky

were alive with the thunder that shook
the corrugated iron. We were wet
with sweat—it was a hundred degrees

that day. Granny said, *hot as bloody Hades.*
It was Christmas time—the girls
were up for holidays—and we were

playing under the verandah. The sun
spread a golden glow in the calm
before the gathering storm

as the first snake of the season
came slithering out of the fowl yard,
leaving us its red-checked skin.

Eurydice and the Tawny Frogmouth

On the low arch
above our gate,
he looks out
through a fringe
of feathers,
hunting,
then places one
foot on black
cast iron and ruffles
his head. His other
foot is clenched
in the night air,
held out
in an atmosphere
of waiting—then
unclenched.
Those nights
flying with you
weighed no more
or less than
this.

Singing His Head Off

He stumbles on a rocking pontoon
at the end of his long wharf,
tying things down—greasy ropes

loop around pylons, old tyres hang
from boats. He was ferryman
at Kangaroo Point before the bridge

was built and his horse and punt
decommissioned—it's all gone
into myth now. His arms almost float

in the humid air, he's barely there.
He coalesces around the feeling of loss
of his wife in his stomach.

She's been underground for a week.
He invited no one to the funeral
and has given up speaking.

Cockatoos in the tall melaleucas
above the graveyard drop seed husks
and shake their sulfur crests.

Standing now with his back to the storm,
he straightens and begins to sing—
a deep low moan building

to a howl and a high elemental
keening—his song that could once
make rocks weep.

Eurydice, After a Midnight Storm

A koel glides from a nest
abandoned by owls.
We wade in a tide
of humidity. Blue
morning-glory vines
grow in thick night,
undergrowth's stranglers.
The storm breaks
and moves out to sea.
I smell you in the calm
air, an edgy presence,
as house lights
blink on one by one
and Easter's garbled noise
is switched off, then walk
to the edge of the river
and listen to the tide
rush downstream.

Eurydice in Sydney

What was he thinking while I was gone?
Was his mind still doing time in his head,
dancing in abstract darkness?

Pain comes and goes. I notice things
I hadn't before: the city ibis stitching its voice
to the wind between car park and George Street.

I think of going shopping with him.
Bogong moths in a shaft of sunlight
flutter beneath the blue trees

of a shadowy Hyde Park. Does
Sydney Harbour still exist? Depends
on how his voice murmurs

late into night as he drinks, rustling
still with that old ardour, trailing ribbons
of smoke and blood.

Eurydice Combs Her Hair

We reach the end of a bay
and cut in through mangroves.
Our boat hits the bottom,
kicks up mud and sand.
Crossing a deep hole,
the water changes texture—
the surface becomes choppy—
and the trees along the shore here
are the colour of salmon fillets.
A whipbird cracks its call
down a sandstone escarpment
as we anchor up and the sun
sets behind clouds. I sing to you,
wherever you are. In the dark's
chill I can smell your hair,
even though you're
beyond reach.

Eurydice on Fire

A shapeless field of mist above the river's
surface, drifting. At first light the head

of a tree emerges, then black sticks
from oyster racks. The mist

parts as it rolls across
a channel pole's yellow marker—

another level of watching settles
in thinking the mist

forms ribbons and leaves
wisps of itself

in mangrove branches.
My head starts burning,

jagging its hurt deeply: here's
a woman caught in time,

unable to grow old.
She's never said a word

I've heard of. Can she speak?
Do I have any choice?

I step clear, fully alight,
for long enough to think

What's to say? Her voice
echoes the absence.

Eurydice Reads 'Roots and Branches'

Torchlight flares on the book's
cover—reading's difficult in the boat—
and you wonder, is the helmsman
distracted by light?
                              On this river
there's only one destination, that dock
on the other side. The pages
are smeared by yellow light-beams:

> *What time of day is it?*
> > *What day of the month?*

We continued the crossing—flowering gums,
bees flying by polarised light—then watched
a shape forming, an emerald blur of wings
at the periphery of torchlight, a bee-eater
hovering over words, over the hive
of the book.
                    We taste honey
on our tongues—an orange beak flashes—
and read to one another in pitch dark,
carried on the wings of words.

Reaching Light

Where was it we left from?
We say the journey's up, but maybe

memory sinks deeper.
Our journey so far

has been quiet, the only
incident being that rock dislodged

as he spun around on his heel.
What was that stuff—brimstone?

The first slice of sunlight glanced off
a slab of dark marble that turned to glow.

His back moved ahead of me—
his curls, shoulders,

that neck. What new bone was he inventing
in his shuffling head, what chance

that a doorway would appear and then a house?
The dark supported me, comfortably

behind me, a cradle woven from
demon hair. As I rose

and climbed toward day, his turning head,
those eyes—strips of memory,

silver tides, moons rising over the
rim of the world—

brought back the day we were married,
standing in fine rain, then escaping from family,

sex by a rolling surf in a high wind, velvet
heavens and the stars omens:

calendars, clocks, zodiacs—
straight, bent signs

NEW POEMS

࿘

Juno
You taught me how to weigh the harvest of light

The Kingfisher's Soul

A wave hits the shoreline of broken boulders
explodes, fans into fine spray, a fluid wing,
then drops back onto the tide: A spume
of arterial blood. Our eyes can be gulled by what
the brain takes in—our spirits take flight
each time we catch sight out—feathers of smoke
dissolve in air as we glide towards clarity.

In the old days I used to think art
that was purely imagined could fly higher
than anything real. Now I feel a small fluttering
bird in my own pulse, a connection to sky.
Back then a part of me was only half alive:
your breath blew a thicket of smoke from my eyes
and brought that half to life. There's no

Evidence, nothing tangible, and no philosopher
of blood considering possibilities,
weighing up feathers, or souls. One day
some evidence could spring from shadows
as my body did in rejecting the delicious poisons,
the lure of dark song. You came with a wind
in your gaze, flinging away trouble's screw,

Laughing at the King of Hell's weird command;
you created birthdays and the cheekbones
of family—I was up, gliding through life
and my fabrications, thought's soft cradle.
I scoured memory's tricks from my own memory,
its shots and score cards, those ambiguous lyrics—
clear bird-song was not human-song, hearing became

Nets and shadowy vibrations, the purring
air, full of whispers and lies. I felt blank pages,
indentations created by images, getting by
with the shapes I made from crafted habits.
You taught me how to weigh the harvest of light.
There was bright innocence in your spelling,
I learned to read again through wounded eyes.

Wispy spiders of withdrawal sparked with static
electricity across skin, tiny veins, a tracery of
coppery wires, conducting pain to nerve
patterns: all lightweights, to your blood's iron.
You brought along new light to live in
as well as read with—before you came, whenever
I caught a glimpse of my own blood, it seemed

A waterfall of bright cells as it bled away.
The clouds of euphony, created by its loss, became
holes in thinking, pretend escape hatches. You're now
a rush, wings through channels of my coronary
arteries. We slept together when you conjured
a bed in your Paddington tree-house: barbless hours,
peace appeared and said: Soon, the future awaits you.

I stepped into the day, by following your gaze.

The White-bait

The first winter frost
burns delicate leaves
of basil in terracotta pots,

coats the kangaroo-paw
ferns; white fur collars
on crimson buds.

The hardy starlings
flit about, pecking dirt;
singing, click, click.

I read the morning news
and then think of
the unblinking eyes

of silver gulls—
their beaks slash at
white-bait still kicking

in plastic boxes on the wharf
of the Fisherman's Co-op.

In our garden, a patch
of sunlight moves across
the grass, eating the crystals of ice.

Brush Turkey in the Cold Room

for Anthony Lawrence

At the Fisherman's Co-op
I stand in the cold room and look out the window's
scale-plastered glass, the river's being
whipped up by a westerly, chop cuts across
the ferry's prow and brakes into white spray.

Someone's hung a *no smoking* sign in the freezer.
We puffed our way through the best days of our lives,
and shortness of breath didn't bother us.

Dutch walks up from the pontoon with a box
of dusky flathead, the neon light from the hood
of the freezer flares all around his hair—
He's a classic *cast the net on the other side*
sort of bloke—he shovels flakes of ice
onto his catch, then lights up a rollie, at 50
he's still strong as a White Ox—'*We spend our life
waiting—lines, fish, love and money and in no order,
whatever comes up first*'—he repeats every time he drinks.

A brush turkey walks into the cold room,
glances sideways, and stupidly, senses no danger—
Dutch keeps shoveling ice—its tail a black fan
vertically held, its wattle bright as orange antifouling paint.

My Grandfather's Ice Pigeons

My grandfather would walk into the house,
on a summer evening after his work, then empty
his catch of mud crabs into the bathtub;
they'd flow out in a stream of ice-flurry from
his four-gallon drums, then settle in a heap of
black and olive speckled claws, spiky legs
and back flappers waving frantically. One night
my mother caught me holding a broomstick
with an angry muddie's claw clamped around it.
She ordered me to stay away from the crabs
reminding me why Uncle Eric lost his finger;
they could even snap a clothes prop in two.
My mother went back to the city. I stayed
a week and my grandmother showed me
what to do, first throw one into a bucket of ice
to slow it down, then bind the claws together
with kingfisher-blue twine in a slipknot.
Old Dutch would come to take them
to the Co-op in his truck, packed into fish boxes
covered with ice. My grandfather would leave
again for his next catch, he'd take some pigeons
with him in a cage on his trawler. If he
had a good haul, he'd let one of the birds go,
when it came home it was my job to ride my bike
into town to order the ice. When I reached
the Co-op, Dutch would ask how many pigeons?
If more than one, it was a box of ice a bird.

He'd send the ice to my grandfather next morning
on the mail boat. They talk about the time
Fa Fa got drunk up the river at Spencer,
the river postman saw him through the mist
one morning, balancing on net-boards at the stern
of his boat, singing aloud, throwing pigeons at the sky.

The Lakeside Rituals

Drive through the town, don't stop
at the hotel, pass the marlin with its neon sword,
notice the pelicans perched
on the streetlights, pull up and park
by the lake. It's the dark of the moon
and the bulrushes smell of burning kerosene.

Men wade through lake water,
follow children who lead the way
with flaming wicks, they are scoop-netting prawns.
They arrived with their families
in cars and trucks, some bring tents.
Behind drawn blinds in the caravan park

husbands get drunk or slip away.
When the last group comes in with their catch,
fires glow in red-hot drums—
they boil buckets of salt water
and play country music or rock.
They do a kind of dance, not really dancing,

attending to rituals, sometimes
a fist-fight will break out, or even a stabbing
may happen. It's mainly a double-shuffle
and a song. Then they feast on the catch—
peeling prawns and drinking beer,
making toast or boiling billies as the curlews call.

Ungaretti at Broken Bay

A blue heron, foraging for its young,
circles a stranded cicada—then
stops, assuming a position of aim.
A family of redhead finches
pour out from a hole in a hollow
tree stump of yellowbox.
Cats scavenge for fish heads
by the cleaning slab; water rats
nest under sun-bleached planks
that jut from a mudbank.
The tide's right and Guiseppe
prepares to set his long lines—
He throws out the kellick:
when it takes a grip on the bottom
the traces will follow, with their
butterflied fillets of mullet,
pinned to hollow-point 5.0 hooks—
these baits, still seeping blood,
will flutter through the water column.

Narkissos on a
Game-fishing Boat

The surface of the river
caught by an eddy
and the clipping
wing of a westerly wind

crazed mirrors
in every leaping wave
reflecting cubist
faces on each edge

the water lapping
on the side of the boat
hissing and coughing
catbird songs

at the river's mouth
where sweet water
meets the salt
tide's lapping tongue

I listen to echoes
in the hull as the V8
thrums drunk on petrol
fumes and calling

for more dark music
the sunlight shatters
reflections and the white
foam of the wave hits home

The Net

after József Attila

Curly hair's thinning, dry flakes
drift around my shoulders—
I've lost my fountain pen again.
Uncle Eric, the family's last professional
fisherman, is dead. Don't worry
though, I'm not alone.

I trawl my bloodstream
and nerves, my genetic fishing net,
in these dark waters
catch a few sparks of light—
my mesh's torn, so I hang it up
and grab a needle.

Now my net's hung out
on the clothes line, I can see
translucent scales, white twigs
from swayback river gums; twisted knots
of hair from ribbonfish tails,
stars in a firmament.

The Fledglings

They came ashore, human dregs from the ferry,
some of the men hauling cages on long poles.
The imprisoned calls of birds caught in wakes
of air at the back of the smugglers' heads.

Then they moved along the avenue and passed
before the window; I sat in my workshop
cutting patches of cloth that no longer held
the wind—to be used as flags on fishing boats—

They came each afternoon, trudged
over the cobblestones, their heels clicking
as the first koels of summer made their piercing calls.
Night held the promise of white asparagus

on the shore, iron-rich seaweed at the mouth
of the bay. On dark nights I longed to converse
about the brain-fever birds—there was no interest
until you came, with your ear for

the right nuance as it vibrated across
acoustic threads of talk. These words seek
the delicate vessel once called the soul,
so take care my love, or they may stitch one—*flag-like*—

to the back of your head. These birds,
so highly audible by day, are rarely seen—who bears
witness to their dark migrations? They arrive in time
for spring, constantly raiding the nests of others.

When brain-fever birds perch, they become
flowering branches in jacarandas—they sing their
two notes and lay soft eggs within thoughts
that fledge inside our heads, as a longing for flight.

In Winter Night

❧ *for Pat Dobson*

Though I call across the water no sound rings out
river's escarpments spines of sandstone books
written in a cryptic alphabet
shaped from the movement of twigs in the trees
when I step away from myself
I speak in the voices of night birds
move out from my body into the air above the tide
and hover between the river and night sky
Whose voice comes out of my mouth
never mine when I enter this bay
where I mimic the voice of water fowl
a voice used by the river people
before my grandfather's wooden hull and stroking oars
and my motor and fiberglass
Whose voice returns in a wood-duck's throat
some avenging hunter who shakes
the page of ownership and says we belong
written on rock the old songs
watched as the cliffs crumbled away
the music that rose up from the earth
was the shredded voices of crows
whatever they were called   they walked
differently   with other ways of crying
We came and polished the surface of the river
and holystoned the rock as if it was a deck
chained feathers to breast-plates
filled wings with lice-killing powders
we watched the diamond fire-tail finches in clouds
waiting for the seed-eaters to enter their long extinction
with our nets and our guns on our shoulders

Pied Butcher Bird Flute Solo

I steer at full throttle, the boat lifting up
onto the plane, shooting past
Dead Horse Bay, straight under
the bridge and into the upper reaches
of the river. We glide the surface
of the incoming tide, I want to
make it to my marks on time—
now a great white sponge of fog
has come down around us,
it dampens my hair and suddenly
reduces visibility. I cut the motor
and we drift with the tide which takes
the boat close into the shore.
The river narrows and there's eucalyptus
in the atmosphere. Silent now
and almost blind. The fog envelops us.
At first, a few wobbly notes
coming from all sides, a deep-throated
fluting climbing the bird-scales,
it loops into a theme, then notes cascade
into a melody that drifts over
the silk of the surface, under the rolling
blanket of fog. So lovely a song
it almost sounds like human-whimsy
becoming a liquid bubbling,
almost a blue yodel, the ghost of Jimmy
Rodgers, then fades again.
A few plopping splashes, mullet
hitting the cotton-wool air above them
and landing with belly flops.

We drift silently until a cricket
kicks in with a high, nervous drone
for a thin moment. Almost silence awhile
until that murderous avian spirit
player resumes the masterpiece—
now concert flute, mellow-toned
with a sort of back-beat, an amplified pulse
underneath its sweet mock carolling.

Looking into a Bowerbird's Eye

Untamable, fluttering, a feathery
cold pulsing in my hands—
A mature male bowerbird.
House-glow, the night outside,
here the kitchen light reflects
electric splinters, uncountable
shards clustered in a blue eye.
Everything flares to a beak
pecking at fingers, claws
raking the palm of my hand,
alembic depths of blue eye-tissue.
He was trapped in a cupboard at 3 a.m.:
the cat's voice woke the house.
Fingers flecked with specks
of blood now, the eye
a fiery well of indigo cells, cobalt,
ultramarine, cerulean blues.
A pale moon slips through
tree branches outside—
the window pane frames its quarter,
then a squall of refracted
light in eyes that a human
cannot read—opaque, steadfast.
Light-sensitive molecules, intricate
lenses, a blue cone of tissue.
Outside, bracing night air, the stars
clustered in the milky way—
my hands, opening, flicked by wings.

Double-eyed Fig Parrot

A camellia-scented breeze
parts the shore and bruises the apple I'm eating. My free will
drifts across the river. It's been raining and silver
gulls feast on the sepia run-off.

I've been up all night
in the boat-shed painting my year-long affair with abstraction.
Now I try to write but words stick to my fingers
above the screen's false surface. So I draw instead, with
charcoal on creamy paper: half-formed wings
of teal appear, sketches of talons and beaks. Actual
wings part the air outside and a possum's knocking
simulates a jazz beat on the roof.

One winter morning,
a dealer arrives with a truckload of caged birds. I feast my eyes,
exotic, on the delicate colours of a double-eyed fig parrot.
Have I ever seen one of these creatures before? I make
a few phone calls, discover that no one knows
who I've become. My family suggests a travel cure.

The plane arrives at Perth—
change that to London—in a smudged dawn. I catch a cab to the
nearest hotel in a mood that fogs the light of my room.
When I open the luggage, it contains only a stub
of charcoal, and hundreds of drawings of a single bird,
all the same specimen: a double-eyed
fig parrot.

The Golden Bird

᪾ *for Nathaniel Tarn*

Winter-dusk, darkness closing,
trailing a damp cloak.
Chilling the soft bones of my shoulder's
in-grown wing—pain from
a new wound flickers out—
forking through the rapture of writing,
cold air seeking it.

After reading your book
The Embattled Lyric I feel
closely linked to you—your triple Orpheus,
then Eurydice in all her
changing shapes—
multiple raids on Hades and back
to the light.

Still, these days I prefer
the dark, cold, and a clarity
of mind—even when I feign confusion,
I hold tight to what keeps me
alive—a spur-winged
plover in its broken-wing dance,
distracting the hawk from her chicks—

Sliding into a trance,
I see the waxing quarter
moon as light across a cotton-wove page—
though now, what act of
imagining could create warmth
from reflected light? Nothing,
silence, blind-air, blank.

Blaise Pascal, testing
a theory, decided finally
to invent a vacuum chamber, a device
that might bring a void into being—
his concept's slug-gun?—
(Like Buckminster Fuller building a tetrahedron
at Black Mountain College).

At times literary critics mock
poets who imagine
Orpheus harmonising with lyrebirds,
a bird whose song
can pulsate with variations
on a rival's mating call, singing
a kind of bird-jazz.

Today broken words gather
on pages in a broken time,
does the powerful owl's hooting call hang
in some obscure night,
haunting itself? When the last
owl passes, bitter laughter—
the fisher kookaburra, hooking

snakes up from gutters.
Minerva's owl once spread its
wings at dusk and called aloud on our behalf.
W.B. Yeats's final vision
was a gold clockwork bird
to defeat the abyss. When his heart
stopped, did he believe

it would transcend him:
gold-foil wings hovering
over the void, intricate golden beak singing
eternally—after the world's end
beyond hearing?—Ted Berrigan wrote
'I rage in a blue shirt
at a brown desk in a bright room'—

There's a line by Wallace
Stevens, written in a foul
mood on a grey day in Connecticut: 'the sound
of the mind is an echo.' Outside
the window tonight, a star chart
unfolds, on the pane Narcissus inscribes:
The human miracle?

Joseph Cornell's Tools

Joseph Cornell used these sturdy tools
and instruments to create boxes,
time-machines. Constructions
made from bits and pieces,
three-dimensional frames containing
fans, lace, feathers—other
once ephemeral objects, including
a torn fragment of photography,
an image of Mallarmé's
hands—One contains an illustration
of a hummingbird—it seems
to hover in the space between
the glass and the backing of the box.
In another, an etching
of a great horned owl—like the bird
I watched one night,
perched on a light-post in Boulder,
Colorado: it swoops from
memory, filling my study with silent
flight as I recall another
visitation. This afternoon,
returning from the post office
I drove ahead of an approaching storm,
trees shook and a black cockatoo
flew out of them, it sailed on
just ahead of my car for almost a minute,
a long time given the situation—
stroking the air before the windscreen,
following the road, so close
I could see details of its plumage,
two red patches across the tail feathers.
Something other than beautiful, fleeting.

At Rock River

for Peter O'Leary who drove me to Woodland Pattern, Milwaukee

In a subway in New York City,
Zukofsky carefully watches

a praying mantis on a page
of newspaper in full defensive

display. In a Milwaukee
factory Neidecker listens to workers

on their lunch-break yarning.
Lines drawn, some in books

others in sand—spinning tangles.
Lorine sorting through

her father's lines that hauled carp.
Everything difficult, even

in hours writing lines of poetry
words came a letter at a time,

creating phrases, images
of buckets tipped over with a light

touch, line breaks making
sense of her sparse life—Rock River's

pull. She changed the water
level until she drew Zuk

and Basil Bunting to her front door.
Green tree frogs croaked

and a barn owl cleared the bone
from its throat. Sound of paddle

splash, then a water rat drops down
from the plank-wood

dock to scurry under netboards.
There was her father's bent back

as he pulled them home
along with the shuddering catch:

carp-scales caught in mesh
were silver coins in broad shafts

of the late sun. Night time,
after the dishes, a dream of hands

roughened on oat-sacks.
Dawn, starling chatter and ratshit,

Lorine watches a white moth
on a stalk of blossoming rose mallow.

After the soft crack of duck eggs—
she sits at her breakfast table, writing

lines including factory talk,
her way, until it seems to matter.

Bolinas Bay, an Ode

❧ for Joanne Kyger

At Joanne's, *three* rainbows over the bay.
In the garden, talking, our bird-song and calls,
spun to metaphors in sunlight—

Words, all afternoon, mingled with
their meanings, songs of light, memories of poets
along sempiternal zones in our heads.

Light, an abstract surf, tides of air behind it
hung with Anna's hummingbirds:
their condensed flight, the sound of Joanne's

thought—garden trees turned their leaves,
showing veins, pencil-traces of her handwriting
from the 1960s. One day back then

lashing out, she parodied an elder's poem
read it to class—boys in tight with themselves—
her words danced above their heads,

jazz-notes. A moth flutters around a light shade,
leaving traces of silver powder on the globe—
the desire for something afar—I look out

and catch sight of a troupe of blue jays
on a foray into what was left of their day.
Joanne turns in her kitchen, radiating within,

opening her intellect's wings. Memory's atomic
particles collide, sparks glow in Joanne's pupils,
her energies, packing a punch.

Through glass, the first woodpecker I've ever seen,
it slices and chops into a tree trunk
uncovering worms in their cocoons.

Inside Robert Creeley's 'Collected Poems'

We learned from *After Mallarmé*, beyond thought's reach
    there was a silence in stone,
a compression of dry language without music, then we began
    to understand difference
between sex in our heads and sex in the bed; the form of
    women a way to hold chaos,
that singing bird, in a cage we imagined you had projected just
    ahead of vision where eyes

remembered a look that killed, our unbelieving bodies listened
    too long to the music
of stone. There were sails waiting in the harbour, oceans
    beyond the beaches and nighthawk moons,
walks along coastlines where the great redwoods stood
    recording us then a loop
in time talking all night with Augustine in Hippo 'a projection
    of the mind'.
All of Africa, in a '67 Mustang down Highway 61 on a river of
    prose as ideas were soaked
by forgotten monsoons as the world guttered into your voice
    reciting *The Garden*
in a half empty classroom, you recounting afterward yourself
    as a young man
breeding Birmingham Rollers.

The stage without props but shadows with a woman who
    played out the role,
a classic one-act show repeating stage directions instead of
    lines, her despairing husband
off-stage as a tape-loop, as a wet crow at a crossroad, feathers
    black ink smudging words
in the examinations, your regret bound in so tightly by your
    lines—so it could not leach
away as a guilt pool. We passed those desert mountains and
    fourth time round you made
more songs delicate music with flashes of anger stashed for the
    mornings after.

The piled up manuscripts adrift in kitchens of light your
    relentless questions probing
the ones who loved you, beating your hand and repeating over
    the word 'heart'
until its meaning bruised the hearts that loved. Possible
    meanings returned in *The Finger*,
your tool and your weapon, splitting lines with a ballpoint,
    tearing the flesh, the paper,
the page, the personal pronoun stranded then as father to
    children belying kindness
as you'd pad the floor of bedrooms chanting madrigals of fierce
    love.

No shoes, no issues, no re-writes —and you singing inwardly at
    the door to the gallery,
gliding along through painted skies, the poem taking us into,
    and then out the other side
of the book, laying down lines, word by word on billowing
    sheets waking dreams
three-dimensional worlds, alive. The printer setting slugs of
    type your smoke proofs
spelling out the need for a high morale, a way to live the words,
    yes 'tell 'em it's fun let's go!'
 Although we sit here at the table stunned by time: The Creels'
    maps spread out
across the floor of the tent.

From the hills above Bolinas Bay the turkey vultures hang in
    the clear sky, black handkerchiefs,
parachuting pages—the sky's false Indulgences, while you live
    on, as long as we listen,
and there's no reason to repent.

Blues for James McAuley

He walked to nurse a breakdown, water
lapped his toes, the shine of the beach received him.
A seahorse swam upright in a rock pool.

As he walked he peeled off skins.
The fin of a grey nurse shark cut through the foam
as this man flew his soul like a kite,

and prayed for absolution,
then reeled it right back in again.
The waves churned pine cones at his feet.

Straps of kelp stained the white sand.
'I'll drink with the Devil and smoke with God'
he told his class as they mocked his jazz.

He walked on singing his own lyrics to the tune
of 'Annie Laurie' and watched a school
of parrot fish undulate like bad sex

manipulated by men in Rome.
The surf washes up a wounded fairy penguin—
Peeling off another skin, an idea sunk home:

Lion Island—he struck out across the bay
where prison ships sailed in formation.
Red crabs sidled up the rocks claimed by England,

killer prawns edged in. After sunset, he dropped
into a hospital at South Head to study X-rays
of his heart—more he looked, darker it became.

He preferred a nurse to a fairy penguin.
The sandstone island tucked its paws away.
He walked on, calling Annie Laurie by her name.

Black Laughter, Budapest 1934

᷽ after József Attila

It's summer, it's a fine evening.
The trains rattle through the station,
you can hear the knock-off horns
blaring from the factories,
coal-stained roofs are stained again
by the black night, under
the streetlights the newsboys
yell headlines, cars zip
and skid on the tramlines
the trams clang one after the other
neon signs flair until you
start to go blind by reading them,
in the back lanes the walls
caked with last week's posters
lean in and stifle your last impulse
to laugh it off—men with
faces straight from cartoons hurry
away from others who want
to hold them back, the necks
of the avenues are stiff with anger.
You can hear the trudging
footsteps of workers heading home
as if they were old mystics
walking to nowhere on this earth.

You can even hear the soft
wrists of pickpockets whispering
between coats, right beside
a man from the country who sighs
as if he's just thrown a stack
of hay onto a cart. I listen to it all,
the beggar who quietly
simpers and wipes his nose,
the woman who looks sideways
for a second or two—
she knows that I'm a stranger here,
so I just sit on a doorstep
and keep my mouth tightly closed.
It's summer, it's a fine evening.

Black Laughter, Sydney

It was twilight in a rowing boat on Sydney Harbour.
Out from Blues Point, I was pulling hard
on the oars of a hired rowboat to be
returned before the natural curfew of darkness—
This was over thirty years ago and memories
are complex things—one image is stronger
than the others, flying foxes moving in black files
across the sky above the harbour, flying
out from my childhood into their present
continuing for a million years or so.
This memory comes back each time my resolve
to keep my soul free from stain weakens,
even for a moment: the bats, the determined
pulling on the oars. A westerly wind
was chopping up the harbour, wakes from
ferries slapped against the wooden skiff,
I was wet to the skin and bailing out with a can.
When I made it to the Quay I found
myself walking through a crowd of people
who were smartly dressed and eating cold canapés.
It was a reception for a triple marriage,
three brides and their grooms married under
the sails of the Opera House, there were comments
about real estate and flying fish. On the corner
of the street a busker swung a bullroarer
and handed round a hat, two cops in a V8 car
parked at the kerb revved up the motor in time
to the homeless man's blunt instrument.

A woman explained this whole event
had been hexed by some witch in Kings Cross—
A pigeon-fancier offered news that predators
lived high in the city's glass canyons—each night
raptors swooped to kill the road-peckers,
along with racing birds still homing though the dusk.
It was twilight in a rowing boat on Sydney Harbour.

Autumn, Europe 1943

♪ after Miklós Radnóti

Seen through steel-coloured clouds, the sun
rises higher and the sky tears itself in two—
a blue flag, a stained shirt cloth.
Poisonous vapours bank up and absorb
the sun's warmth. Below them, we notice
a swallow setting out to leave—we can faintly
hear its call—more like a thin scream.

On the rubble, what's left of the graveyard wall,
a red lizard scuttles. In the air, a live cargo
from autumn's legacy: carnivorous wasps.
On the banked earth, makeshift trenches, men
sit staring at distant fires of death. We can
smell the rot as it settles down through the air.
The dry bracken smoulders, setting free

a swirling eddy of sparks, this flares into flames
from the fiery wind. The coming dark will
illuminate more calligraphy of burning.
In vineyards, grapes shrink to ruined sultanas,
vines wither and their dry yellow flowers
crackle in wind, dropping seeds onto
the burning ground. Whole fields are beginning

to sink into this sea of smoke and mist.
We hear an insane clattering of huge carts
that shake what's left of the leaves off the branches
of ancient trees. Look my love, there
in your hair, a golden leaf, fallen from a branch
shaking above your head. Everything's starting a drift
into exhausted sleep, but wait, look

there's death, finally lovely in its glide down
the valley as the sky cradles what's left of the garden.
One last wise move, together, let's love each
other then lean into sleep. Out there, the thrush
has been asleep for a while, kiss me now, fall with me.
The walnuts fall onto the piles of dead leaves
without making a sound. And reason falls apart.

The Guard's Advice

∿ after reading René Char's Les Matinaux

          An hour before dawn   set down   moths flutter
     from the letterbox   diamond-winged white-tipped
        fly in circles   around a match flare
our world a match flare   the particular
           moth's whiskers trembling   feathery antennae
receiving what moths   receive   moth talk
            a Parisian radio station   in the background
no news   take-over talk   back to the grass
     in my region   here now the sun comes
warms my cheeks   even though   just yesterday
            I cursed the heat   then as shadows   lengthened
I thought shadows might be some   kind of protection
     until they became damp   and clung to us
               shadow-nets   shadow splotches   undergrowth
a fish gasping by a river   the water-stained   tea-coloured
     a capsized boat   two bodies   and bees
             in the rushes   bees still able   to sting
hanging around too long   for anything   weakens faith
      I waited for her   three months   she was impatient
           for mercy   she wanted to break away
rather than go stale   in the ruins of a school
        a doorstep in the freezing pre-dawn   we made love
a cracked doorstep   wrecked seating on canvas
        on my parachute   black silk   white skin   moths
ants moving on   a tracery of snail-slime
            I stay here in my region   our region   she returns
it seemed ridiculous   in the end   she walked
       through the door   in pain   her wound bandaged
              holding an armful of huge dark roses
         she carried their sweet scent   of velvet decay

        her eyes   carrying images
                of the dyker's abusive hands   skins
    pale our faces the pallor of night   fingernails shot
        cracked then I uncovered the green apples from
a deserted orchard fallen fruit the cold air   biting like a
    vice
        my knife paring away the bruised flesh
            she carried a message   from a German guard
        whispered it he said   *desert*   whatever else
    desert

The Intervention

৵ for Ali Cobby Eckerman

When Yeats writes, *Soul clap its hands
and sing, and louder sing*, it feels tangible,
and yet a friend says we can't use
the word 'soul' these days, but
then adds, all the more reason. When
I heard you reading your poetry
in Castlemaine, a long steady song,
I was breathing the air of your soul,
we were both hundreds of miles from
our own countries, your body swayed
as you called up a whole world,
with images and stories woven
through with suffering. Lines
were licks of lightning, some thin
as the chill of your meanings that
we all recognised—all I can compare
this with is the feeling you get
swimming alongside a shark, or
the shot of joy in watching a lyrebird
shaking out its tail in full display,
pouring *all* song into its own singing.

Summer at Carcoar

ᕚ after the painting by Brett Whiteley

The painter enters   time through the Belubula River,
draws out long bodies   from poplar trees
drenches the air   a Naples yellow hue, polishes water flow
to a waxy sheen   until it sings under glowing light
he turns a bend   a joyous curve and quick line
then moves over   paddocks, back to the place
where he was born   to embrace ideas of chaos, accelerating
particles in his head,   paints original county as a garden
over scars, sketches notes   on the edges, a wren flicks its tail up
and brush strokes freeze   blue feathers onto surface
the willow pulses salicylic acid   through his idea of pain
the shape of particular hurting   just under skin,
a rock where a currawong   becomes larger than it was
in life, running under   tissues in a burrow where flecks
of the past gleam through   a green subterranean light
from a Hades   of childhood's fears
a crumbling   ground of families,
here we notice   an absence of human figures
and intense deciduous   trees glow
and squat under bird song   the sun new pain
rabbits hint at movement,   twitch in grasses
details load themselves :   golden paddocks
made up in the mind,   river a memory spilling
its ballast   hard discoveries, the ground opened
though intricate   eddies in tides of grass
the ten thousand   brush strokes, branches
of thought   etching themselves under the small sky,
feathers   counted, each leaf a fold
wild   patterns so right you believe the painted world

then   sense an open field believes you   while under
ground
around   the boiling core Whiteley's scars
indicate mining,   around 1905 they discovered
uranium here   a local paper called it *the parent of radium*
we sense in the painting's   glow, stains of undertow
a lash in the black highway   as it curves outside the frame
we too sense a marsupial instinct   to tunnel down
and glance flowers, mauve bells   ringing their soft trumpets
then a bee's arc describing flight,   a thought becoming
amber.

Lyrebirds

I went back to see the house I rented
during my factory days. It was here
I saved money for my first
typewriter. The factories have closed
or moved away, except one— a sinister
red-brick building, windowless,
without signs—yet in front, a pole
flying the Australian flag.
I parked and listened to the muffled
sounds of light industry,
then watched the workers file out
after their shifts, the younger
men loitering around a parking lot.
Some looked like the old gang,
ruthless delinquents. I beckoned
and one of them walked up to my car.
I asked what happened inside
and he replied, 'First, we attach copper wings,
then spot-weld aluminium scrolls
for the tails, we don't muck about,
there's money in lyrebirds these days.'

Praise and Its Shadow

Standing on this rocky shore
at the end of the point, sun's
hitting sandstone escarpments as it sinks,
colouring everything red—
I watch the felty black surface
of the river carrying pelicans
downstream to the mouth.
I could easily disappear into
this landscape, become
a fisherman again and work
the tide through the moon's cycles
and its darks, pierced with stars—
A local Novalis, courting
the night itself—my nets always
coming in without a catch,
at dawn each new day my head full
of emptiness, nothing there
but love for the long, echoing darkness.

Death of a Cat

Siamese seal-pointer, ghost cat.
My familiar and killer,
sleeper under covers.
A true carnivore
devoured hundreds of pilchards
maybe thousands,
and many baby brown snakes.

That pair of kingfisher bodies.
First the pale female,
jumped and tortured.
Then the male
who returned to help his mate
and met death by tooth and claw.

Roller of lizards and skinks,
blue-eyed and sleek.

Bully-boy with a foul tongue,
most articulate at night.
Shiny, cream-furred cuddler,
brown-eared stalker.
Attention-seeker and bird-watcher.
My wife's tormentor.

The one who ate a dozen
live garfish whole,
stolen from the bait-tank.
Taut-bodied, razor-footed climber
with sprung-rhythm.
Stuck among branches yowling.

Ripping the chairs apart,
while purring for praise.
A 'legend' according to my son,
to my wife, a demented prowling beast

My darling and terrible
King Tut, who prowled here
for eighteen years, before The Mower
cut out his kidneys.

ACKNOWLEDGEMENTS

This volume was selected and edited by Robert Adamson.

The poems in the section 'New Poems' were written between 2005 and 2008 are published here for the first time in book form.

The author would like to acknowledge the generous support of the Literature Board of the Australia Council during the composition of this book.

Grateful acknowledgement is made to the Literature Board of the Australia Council and to the Cambridge Conference of Contemporary Poetry for funding the author's attendance at the Conference at Trinity College in 1998, and to the Literature Board for funding for his visit to the UK and Ireland in 2004 and his reading tour of the USA in 2006. Also to Flood Editions, Chicago for arranging and organising the American reading tour.

Grateful acknowledgement is also made to the editors and publishers of magazines and newspapers in which some of new poems appeared: *Australian Book Review*, the *Age*, the *Australian*, *Chicago Review*, *Heat*, the *Australian*'s *ALR*, the *Weekend Australian Magazine*, *The Best Australian Poems 2006*, *The Best Australian Poems 2007*, *The Best Australian Poetry 2006*, *The Best Australian Poetry 2007*, *The Best Australian Poetry 2008*, the *TLS* and *Jacket 34* online. 'My Grandfather's Ice Pigeons' was commissioned by Johanna Featherstone for the Red Room Company's 'Pigeon Poetry Project.'

Author's note: I would like to thank Juno Gemes, Devin Johnston, Neil Astley, Anthony Lawrence, Kevin Hart, Martin Harrison and Gig Ryan for feedback during the time I was composing the work in 'New Poems.'

PUBLICATION HISTORY

From *Canticles on the Skin* (1970)

   The Imitator
   The Rebel Angel
   Toward Abstraction / Possibly a Gull's Wing

From *The Rumour* (1971)

   Action Would Kill It / A Gamble
   Passing through Experiences

From *Swamp Riddles* (1974)

   The Beautiful Season
   Drifting through Silence
   The Ghost Crabs
   Goshawk over Broken Bay
   Mondrian: Light Breaks upon the Grail
   A New Legend
   The Night Parrots
   Sail Away
   Things Going out of My Life

From *Cross the Border* (1977)

   The Mullet Run

From *Where I Come From* (1979)

   Fishing in a Landscape for Love
   Growing up Alone
   The Harbour Bridge
   My First Proper Girlfriend
   My Fishing Boat
   My Granny
   My House
   My Tenth Birthday

Tropic Bird
The White Abyss

INDEX OF FIRST LINES

INDEX OF TITLES